The New Asia in Global Perspective

Contents

List of Tables, Figures and Maps

Tables

List of Figures

List of Maps

List of Abbreviations

ADB	Asian Development Bank
AFTA	Asia Free Trade Agreement
AMU	Asian Monetary Union
ANZUS	Australia, New Zealand and the United States
APEC	Asian-Pacific Economic Co-operation
ASEAN	The Association of South-East Asian Nations
ASEM	Asia Europe Meeting
CEO	Chief Executive Officer
CEPD	Committee for Economic Planning and Development
CER	Closer Economic Agreement
CIED	Committee for International Economic Development
EAEG	East Asian Economic Group
EDB	Economic Development Board
EMU	European Monetary Union
EPC	Economic Planning Committee
ESB	Economic Stabilization Board
EU	European Union
HPAE	High-performing Asian Economies
IBRD	International Bank for Reconstruction and Development
IEA	International Education Association
IMF	International Monetary Fund
JETRO	Japan External Trade Organization
MEPE	Mactan Export Processing Zone
MFN	Most Favoured Nation
NAFTA	North American Free Trade Agreement
OEM	Original Equipment Manufacturers
SAARC	South Asia Association for Regional Co-operation
SME	Small and Medium-sized Enterprises
TAFTA	Trans Atlantic Free Trade Agreement
TIMSS	Test of International Math and Science Studies
WMU	World Monetary Union

| WORFTA | World Free Trade Agreement |
| WTO | World Trade Organization |

Preface

Asia, with its vast land area and long history, is considered to be the womb of human civilization and, at the same time, a great continent on which currently more than half of the world's population lives. The great continent, however, had been exploited economically during the nineteenth and twentieth centuries, losing its initiative in the turbulent aftermath of the technological revolution ignited by the Gunpowder Revolution. However, following the end of the Second World War, Asia made a brilliant comeback with what has aptly been dubbed 'the economic miracle'. Building on its strong economic strength, Asia is poised to lead the world in creating a new civilization and driving technological innovation. All factors indicate that the millennium from the year 2000 will be led by Asia.

The concept of Asia first originated in Europe. The East and the West have totally different views on the definition of Asia. Europeans, since they conveniently regarded what lies across the Bosporus as being Asia, included Turkey, Arabia and Persia (Iran) in the range of Asia. Referring to Korea, Japan and China as the Far East also stems from a European-orientated world view. Ironically if seen from the perspective of these 'Far Eastern' countries, Europe would be 'Far West' and the USA the 'Far East'.

Such a dichotomy of dividing the world into Asia and Europe, with the Bosporus and the Urals at the centre, has stemmed entirely from a European way of thinking. The Muslims that Europeans categorize as Asians have little in common, and have rarely come in contact with Asians throughout history. Rather, throughout history, Muslims have maintained contact with Europeans and these continuous interactions strongly influenced development on both sides. Therefore, it is more appropriate to view the Islamic culture as being part of the Western culture in a broader sense.

It is more realistic to classify the world into several cultural spheres based on cultural tradition and the degree of interaction rather than on a meaningless geographical method of classification.

In this vein, what divides Europe and Asia should be India, not the Bosporus. If the world is classified from a religious point of view, it is realistic to include new Asia in the non-Islamic western Pacific range. Therefore it is appropriate to include Australia and New Zealand in the expanded definition of East Asia, which ranges from India to Japan.

It does not seem proper to call Australia and New Zealand Asian countries, because the two countries have until recently insisted on the principle of 'White Australia'. After abandoning this principle, however, these countries have pushed aggressively for the liberalization of their respective immigration policies, thereby gradually increasing their Asian population. Moreover, considering their geographic vicinity and economic dependency, the two countries should be included in Asia. Australia, in particular, is gradually becoming an integral part of Asia, since its trade volume with Asia amounts to two-thirds of its total trade and the proportion is expected to grow. In the process of their Asianization, the two countries will be able to gain more economic momentum, cultural diversity and creativity.

In this context, I will define New Asia as the whole region between Japan and India, including Australia and New Zealand. Considering the dynamics of Asia's economy, the definition that expands the concept of the traditional East Asian region should be regarded as being reasonable. Previously, Myanmar was considered to be the boundary of East Asia, and India was classified as a South-west Asian nation. However, India is not only a subcontinent in itself, separate from the Islamic civilization, but it has also been interacting continuously with East Asia, with its Buddhist civilization, for more than 2000 years. Recently, India has recorded growth in trade with East Asia and increasingly considers itself to be part of Asia. Taking all these points into account, therefore, it would be reasonable to classify India as a New Asian nation.

If India is reclassified, New Asia will become home to 28 billion people, more than half of the world's population. Part of the reason for such a population concentration stems from Asia's geographical advantages. Since Asian countries are located in the monsoon region, abundant rainfall gives them an agriculture- and habitation-friendly environment. Also, the Asian population has not decreased much through war or mass killings, since its traditional religions, such as Buddhism, Confucianism, Taoism and Hinduism, are non-violent and order-respecting.

Large population and economic dynamics are not the only reasons this book focuses on the role of Asia in global economic integration. What is more crucial here is the harmony and tolerance of its history and spiritual culture. In resolving conflicts or confrontations, Asians induce their opponents to succumb rather than destroy them completely, and they are more tolerant of different religions or cultures. Furthermore, a desire for economic development has been strong among Asians in the 1990s, and such spiritual energy will be translated into continued growth for a considerable amount of time.

Asia now faces the dawn of a new millennium in which the new rules of the game will prevail. Asia already accounts for 37 per cent of the world's economy. Most economists project that within twenty years, more than half of the world economy will be dominated by Asia. For this to become a reality, war must be prevented at all costs, even the most trivial conflict in the region. The West's uneasiness about the rise of Asia was unveiled in *Culture Clash*, a book in which Samuel Huntington predicted possible clashes among cultures.

Unlike most economic books that concentrate on short-term economic phenomena, this book will trace history back to the Mongol Conquest, a landmark event that reshaped Asia. Since then the mainly agricultural peoples of Asia have been accumulating their national energies while suffering under constant oppression by alien forces. For example, the Yuan and Ching dynasties of China were put under the rule of the Mongols, a comparatively small group of nomads; and Korea, a tenth of whose population were taken prisoner, was almost completely conquered in the process. Japan twice succeeded in fending off Mongol invasions, thanks to timely typhoons. The Japanese call typhoons *kamikaze*, meaning 'God's wind'. Kamakura Bakuhoo, Japan's last feudal government, collapsed as a consequence of the attempted invasions. Hundreds of years of civil war followed the collapse and ended with Japan's reunification, which heightened the country's momentum towards invading the Korean peninsula, and causing the collapse of the Chinese Ming dynasty.

I would also like to explain systematically what enabled the Asian countries to achieve the dramatic economic growth they have in such a short period of time, and suggest ways of applying that unique growth model to the Third World. By reviewing the current economic situation in Asian countries, this book suggests actions to be taken to make Asia a region of dynamic growth, defines its place in world history, and provides a vision for a new millennium.

Some economists, such as Paul Krugman, have a negative view of Asia's economy and potential, suggesting that it has reached its limit of growth since expansion was made possible only by increases in labour and capital investment – a view stemming from a lack of understanding of Asia.

Asian countries have free market economies. Even when their currencies are devalued and their growth becomes stagnant, they have the potential to continue to improve their efficiency. Japan recorded staggering growth up to the 1980s through massive capital investments. Even when high wages and exchange rates affected Japan, it improved its efficiency dramatically by transferring its production lines to South-east Asia, restructured its industries and invested heavily in research and development. As other Asian countries are gradually developing their economies, they are going through similar processes. This book will correct both overly pessimistic or optimistic views about Asia, and help the reader to better understand the past, present and future of Asian economies.

MYUNG-GUN CHOO

Part I
Introduction

1

The Emergence of New Asia and its Historical Significance

Oppression by foreign forces and accumulation of reactionary energy

National enthusiasm for and consent regarding national development are the driving forces of economic growth. Asia's passion for development is the result of a long period of incessant invasion and exploitation by foreign forces, starting with the Mongol conquest in the thirteenth century. When the heterogeneous Mongol tribe destroyed the Chinese Sung dynasty and conquered neighbouring countries, the independent vitality of the mainly agricultural Asian society was temporarily depleted. Inside the apparently strong empire constructed by the Mongol tribe, indigenous agricultural tribes were being exploited and oppressed, and lost their desire to create.

A heightened spirit of independence, as a reaction to the Mongol conquest, led to the formation of a single cultural sphere by solidifying ethnic groups in China which had been preoccupied with hostility and struggle between themselves. The Mongol conquest expanded the geographic boundaries of China and reinforced the central government, giving Asia a totally different face from before.

Mongol invasions of Japan on two occasions, successfully fended off, nevertheless brought about the collapse of the Kamakura Bakuhoo, a Japanese feudal government. A lengthy period of civil war ensued, which ended with reunification process initiated by Oda Nobunaka. The Gunpowder Revolution was the decisive factor in determining Japan's great victory in the Nakashino battle in 1575, when it utilized mass-produced muskets, first introduced by Portuguese merchants. However, before complete reunification of Japan could take place, Oda died during an attack by one of his men, Akechi Mitsuhide. Oda was succeeded by Toyotomi Hideyoshi and Tokugawa Ieyasu, who continued to carry out his various measures for reform. It was during their time that the reunification of Japan was completed. During its drive towards reunification, Japan began to realize the full potential of its power and further armed its military with deadly muskets. In an extension of its reunification efforts, Japan invaded the Korean peninsula in 1592. The Chinese Ming quickly dispatched forces to help the Chosun Dynasty defend itself against the invasion. While the invasion ultimately ended in Japan's defeat, it created an opportunity for the Manchu tribes to unify China by overpowering the militarily depleted Ming.

Ching, a nation established by the Manchu tribe, absorbed Manchuria and the Maritime Province of Siberia, and conquered Inner and Outer Mongolia, thereby greatly expanding Chinese territory. During this process, China, which was at the time under the rule of the Han tribe, and its neighbouring countries, lost their national powers and were easily dominated by the infiltrating Western forces. However, the alien rule ultimately made it possible for the ruled to accumulate more energy for development, by facilitating their unity. This is a similar phenomenon to that which emerged during the founding processes of the Roman and Mongol empires.

While the Western rule of Asia, which began in 1840 with the Opium War, left Asian people ashamed and helpless for up to century, it also promoted national consciousness and rekindled a strong desire in the Asian people to establish their own nations. As a result, post-second World War Asia re-emerged as a completely different cultural entity than before.

A causal nexus of power/science and technology/ economic power

There is a single thread that runs through the turbulent stream of world history beyond time and across borders, namely that power has been a main determinant of social structure. Law and polity have also been transformed basically by interactions between science and technology, and economic and military power. These interactions have also influenced people's sense of values. Even the criterion for feminine beauty has changed over time. During the golden age of Egypt, African women were considered to be the epitome of beauty. At the height of the Greek civilization, the Mediterraneans were the standard of beauty, and since the beginning of the modern era, Northern Europeans have become the standard. Like it or not, in reality, power has exerted a profound influence on human society. The development of science and technology determines the nature of power, and that power transforms social structure, ways of thinking, and the economy. For its part, the economy expedites scientific and technological development, and such development gives birth to a different kind of power. In such interactions of cause and effect, military power, science and technology, changes of thinking, and economic power have worked as agents in the evolution of history. In this context, megaeconomics will function as a window to the future by analyzing systematically how science, technology and power interact to change human thinking.

Gunpowder completely overthrew the political structure of Europe in the late fifteenth century. The newly-introduced firearms broke the power balance where defence had dominated offence, thereby changing the ruling system. In Europe at that time, a small number of well-trained cavalrymen were able to dominate a large number of foot soldiers, mainly farmers, and feudal lords were able to maintain control in every region. The common tactic of the time had been to defend against enemy attack by building a fort and then counter-attacking later. In 1494, however, an impregnable fortress was devastated in just a few hours by the French army led by Charles VIII, and this event started the 'Gunpowder Revolution'. Gunpowder conclusively placed offence over defence, and enabled Europe to witness the end of the feudal system and the rise of the nation-state, and ultimately enabled it to dominate the world.

Although the Chinese invention black gunpowder had been around for a long time prior to 1494, it was this European event that triggered the revolution and led to the subsequent overhaul of Europe's political and economic systems. The following changes were brought about by gunpowder in Europe during that time.

Birth of centralist nation-states

As war became more violent and large-scale with the improvement of arms, small feudal states led by lords became incapable of sustaining war. Also, small-scale nations could not help but be absorbed by political units that had completed integration and become far stronger through their increased economic power. This led to the end of decentralized feudal nations and the birth of strong, centralist nation-states. The number of small independent political entities in Europe dwindled from about 500 in the sixteenth century to about twenty-five around the First World War.

The domination of the world by Europe

Major powers in Europe, with the help of their economic and national strengths dramatically increased by the Industrial Revolution, rushed to secure raw materials and markets for their products. They made determined efforts to colonize Asian and African countries by mobilizing huge vessels equipped with cannons. In 1914, Europeans ruled up to 84 per cent of the Earth, and the area controlled by the UK alone amounted to a quarter of the total. During this brutal colonization process, resisting forces were systematically eliminated, and the military inferior Asian countries were in no position to defend themselves against the European onslaught until the Second World War. With the spread of weapons, however, the world transformed itself into an organically interrelated economic system comprising 185 independent states. Over several centuries Europeans substantially changed the path of historical evolution by colonizing new continents such as the North and South Americas and Australia. It would not be an exaggeration to say that the UK, even with its disadvantages as an island state, was able to surpass the major powers of the old Continent, including France and Germany, with the support of America and the nations of the British Commonwealth, products of its earlier colonization policies.

Class breakdown and changed viewpoints

Unprecedented large-scale war encouraged each European country to adopt a universal conscription system, which necessitated public education to enhance fighting power and productivity of resources. Widespread formal education enlightened the general public, and the idea of equality triggered social reform, thus promoting civil rights. The feudal society, where the concept of wealth mainly meant land ownership, collapsed and central governments began to work with capitalists in order to meet the high price of their bid for power. With the increased importance of money as a device for sustaining a government system, changed viewpoints spread to all walks of life. Above all, theology witnessed the breakdown of the taboo on usury, which had been upheld for centuries.

Even the Christian churches, synonymous with love and servitude, had owned many slaves from ancient times. Kindness was the only religious consideration given to the slaves. Churches, the biggest landowner since the late-Roman era, had used slavery labour to cultivate their vast land. The minimization and popularization of weapons, however, increased the cost of keeping slaves and effectively ended the slavery system.

Meanwhile, Protestant leaders, including Martin Luther, John Calvin and Ulrich Zwingli criticized luxurious churches and built simple and austere ones. They also encouraged people to save, and actively supported the practice of receiving interest for money lent. These changes lifted the religious burden from capitalists and made it possible for them to amass larger capital. This accumulated capital would later result in the Industrial Revolution, which was triggered by the invention of the steam engine.

Redistribution of wealth and enhanced productivity

Gunpowder opened the door for people to accumulate wealth according to their ability by diminishing the importance of physical power to protect property. Furthermore, those who were diligent but had no time to accumulate capital were disburdened of offering good deeds because, in theology, the emphasis of the salvation of souls was transferred from good deeds to faith. Based on the capital accumulated as such, a new middle class was formed. The poor and lazy could no longer depend only on the good deeds of others and had no other choice but to work hard, which greatly enhanced productivity.

The development of technology

As discussed earlier, the Renaissance and the Reformation were as a whole made possible by the spread of gunpowder. Isaac Newton's theory of gravity, which contributed to the shaping of modern thinking, was also a product of gunpowder. Metallurgy, which had advanced in the course of improving artillery, led to the improvement of optics, which in turn contributed to the invention of the telescope. Telescopes made possible the observation of planetary orbits, and the efforts to explain them led to the development of the law of gravitation and differential calculus.

Scientists succeeded in locating planets precisely using Newtonian physics, and this sense of planetary orderliness greatly influenced people's understanding of the universe. With the introduction of Newtonian physics, people came to view the universe as moving as precisely as a clock, and it was thought that all things in the world were created to move in an orderly way according to God's law. Therefore all the phenomena of the universe came to be widely considered as linearly constituted and predictable.

However, ensuing scientific and technological findings proved that the universe is very uncertain and not linearly constituted. In line with this, religions shifted their interest to the realization of 'Heaven and Earth' from the spiritual understanding of human life. Extended power and the role of governments and businesses drove religious leaders to put more emphasis on social justice rather than on the ultimate justice to be rendered by God, and they began to call on the government instead of God to correct the wrongs of the world.

Faith in science and technology made people believe that governments could, by applying scientific principles effectively to economic management, guarantee material prosperity, create jobs, distribute wealth, and so on. In other words, governments took over a part of God's role. The role newly given to governments, however, had its roots in science, quite different from that of supremacy based on theology as in the past.

In the meantime, scientific and technological discoveries sparked a revolution in people's thinking. The heliocentric theory of Copernicus is a good example. His theory overturned traditional Catholic doctrines which proclaimed that all the heavenly bodies move around the Earth because God created the universe with humans at its centre, which later gave rise to the Reformation. The weakening of the authority of the Catholic Church inflicted a fatal blow on feudal lords, whose basis of rule had been religion, and as a consequence, all the political and social systems collapsed. So the revolution in science and technology opened the door to the possibility of constructing of a new culture through the creative destruction of an antiquated mind set.

It was the Industrial Revolution, provoked by the adoption of a new way of production, which empowered Europe to rule the world with its economic superiority. Progress in aerospace and telecommunications technology not only enabled human beings to overcome spatial constraints but also to think three-dimensionally, a dramatic improvement compared to previous times. The development of aerospace technology in particular put the Earth in its place among the small planets. This change of view caused the people of the world to become more interdependent, thus making the coming of the 'global village' inevitable.

As has been discussed so far, power and economics, with science and technology have interdependently combined to change the course of human society.

The fall of the superpowers

World history clearly shows that a civilization can be sustained only when destructive forces are controlled effectively. However, major changes are occurring with respect to such a paradigm.

Economics of offence and defence

In all ages and countries, the balance in military cost between offence and defence has determined the political systems of a society. When the cost of keeping order is less than that of destroying it, a centralist nation is established, whereas when the centre fails to control peripheral violence, authority is decentralized. As the evolutionary trend of weapons made the cost of establishing authority more expensive than the cost of resisting it, world power started to decentralize.

The rapid scaling down of major technologies

Modern technology reduces the size of organizations and makes weapons cheaper and more precise thus reducing the size of a group that can challenge the central authority. While the cost of quelling civil wars is rising, that of confronting the central authority is falling rapidly – this was the critical reason for the collapse of the

USSR. In 1991 a small number of Afghan rebels neutralized the air supremacy of the USSR when their Stinger missiles, each worth only US$80,000 to US$90,000, downed Soviet fighter-bombers worth tens of millions of dollars. This event has the same historic significance as the beginning of the Gunpowder Revolution in 1494, when the forces led by Charles VIII of France devastated a seemingly impregnable fortress with superior artillery. In the economics of war, the USSR was fighting a losing battle.

Reduced effects of reprisal threats by the spread of nuclear weapons

Contrary to general belief, the end of the Cold War raised the risk of the use of nuclear weapons. Even though the international community has made strenuous efforts to ban or abolish chemical weapons and to curb the spread of nuclear weapons as stated in the Nuclear Non-Proliferation Treaty (NPT) it became more likely that breakaway countries, for example, North Korea, or terrorist groups will mobilize weapons of mass destruction. If a terrorist group were to use nuclear weapons, would the world take its revenge in a similar way?

A nation with strong military power can now no longer ignore small but belligerent countries, for the above reasons, thus bringing to a close the era of the superpowers. Instead, the collective security system will inherit the role of keeping order, and therefore economic war will be fought among countries or blocs.

The information revolution and the rise of Asia

The implications of computers and semiconductor technology for human civilization were most evident in the collapse of Communism. Semiconductor technology replaced expensive, bulky machine parts with small microchips and led to a dramatic improvement in the functions of the products used on a daily basis. Increased efficiency in resource utilization and mass production resulted in lower product costs. Today, even the cheapest wristwatch is much more accurate than the most expensive wind-up watch made in the past. This phenomenon can also be observed in the production of weaponry. Semiconductor technology effectively lowered the cost of super-precise, high-performing weapons that in the past only a handful of powerful countries with technological expertise and economic resources could afford. As a result, even the smallest of nations can obtain these weapons with ease. Hence, the cost of maintaining the balance of power is becoming increasingly expensive.

Also, semiconductor technology gave rise to new types of weapons capable of attacking targets with greater accuracy and destructive power than before. One example is the Stinger missile which can be operated by a single infantryman in the field. Others include the Cruise missiles which travel at a maximum speed of 2500 km/h at low altitude to avoid radar detection before hitting targets with an error of just a few metres, and the so-called smart bombs with a deadly accuracy and enough power to destroy an underground bunker. As was attested during the Gulf War, the power of these precision weapons has effectively tilted the global power balance toward the USA. However, it is impossible for the USA to prevent the spread of conventional weapons by itself. In the long run, the current US-led global order will collapse and the continuous stream of technological innovations will ultimately split the world into blocs. World power structure so constituted makes inevitable the advent of New Asia, a tremendous bloc with an overwhelming population. New Asia, which goes beyond the traditional concept of East Asia and includes India and Australia among its members, as the world's largest economic unit with a population of 2.8 billion will exert a considerable amount of influence on the shaping of world order. Furthermore, if New Asia pursues open regionalism, the synergy of economic integration will be maximized. This will be an important stepping stone for the gradual integration of the world under the spirit of World Trade Organization (WTO).

Meanwhile, the development of aerospace technology will enable humankind to overcome spatial constraints, thus changing the outlook on the universe and expediting the integration of the international community. Electronic communication technology, including the Internet, will effectively break state monopoly on information, and by maximizing the capabilities of the individual, create a more centralized and equal world. In light of these facts, Asia is poised to play an increasingly important role in the global arena. In reality, the proportion of the information industry in

Asian economies is increasing rapidly and, considering the nature of the industry, which requires highly skilled manpower, Asia is very likely to prevail in the future.

What America means to Asia

When America first came knocking on Asia's door, it was as a late-comer among the many imperialist nations preoccupied with securing colonies. After the Second World War, it came in contact with Asia again with a more democratized mindset and more mature system. Though America's change in attitude stemmed from its need to counter the imperialist forces of Japan, the instigator of the Pacific War in the 1940s, the country was transformed into a liberator of Asians and greatly influenced the reshaping of Asia for the next half century.

A number of Asia's leading elite came to understand American culture better while studying in the USA, and they adopted the culture aggressively after becoming the ruling class in their own countries. The government and many organizations in America were generous in providing various kinds of scholarship, subsidies and so on to those who would rise to become future leaders in their respective countries. As the victorious country, America could afford to formulate a long-term global strategy based on affluent productivity, foreign reserves, and an almost limitless capacity in issuing dollar notes. It also felt a need to consolidate Asian countries under its flag when the postwar world order took the shape of confrontation between the USA and the USSR. Against a backdrop of such polarization, two historic events took place in Asia: namely, the Korean War and the Vietnam War.

Asia had been subordinated and exploited unilaterally in West – Asian relations. However, the US – Soviet confrontation structure which manifested itself after the Second World War enabled Asian countries to lay the foundations for economic growth in alliance with free Western countries including the USA. Political and economic alliances in particular entered a new phase after the Korean War and the Vietnam War.

With the Cold War intensifying after the Korean War, America felt the need to empower Asia from a global strategic point of view. In other words, helping Asia to grow strong was in the interests of

America. Since Asian countries were fighting against Communism, the USA could prove the superiority of democracy, and deter the USSR from expanding, by supporting them. In line with this, the USA protected Asian countries under a strong security umbrella and opened up its market to encourage those countries to push ahead with export policy. The sudden increase in demands for materials during the Korean War led to the rebuilding of Japan's economy and revived the country that had been struggling after its humiliating defeat in the Second World War. Also, the growth of the Japanese economy proved to other Asian countries that they were capable of achieving economic growth independent of the Western world and this propelled them to aggressively pursue economic developments of their own.

Threatened by the military superiority of the USSR at its peak just after the Vietnam War, America tried to put pressure on its arch rival by even reaching out to China, and endowed that Communist country with the Most Favoured Nation status after President Nixon's visit to China in 1972. China's impressive economic growth was accomplished largely by the rapid increase in exports to the USA. China stepped on to the world stage while America, as part of its containment strategy, was allying itself with every possible nation in order to stymie the USSR. The Vietnam War made America realize Asia's potential as well as its limits. This war also functioned as a catalyst for the USA to shift its Asian policy. The end of the war reshaped the alliance structure in Asia.

China's dramatic economic development, though briefly interrupted by the Cultural Revolution instigated by conservatives, continued. It was the 56 million overseas Chinese, scattered all over the world, who expedited the already rapid growth of China with their astronomical capital.[1] It was in fact the economic potential of overseas Chinese[2] that aborted the US attempt to blockade and check China economically after the Tiananmen massacre.

While China's economy was recording dramatic growth, the USSR, which had been devoted to the arms race with the USA, split into fifteen republics as a result of its defeat in Afghanistan in 1991, marking the end of the Cold War. After the end of the Cold War, however, the USA came to view old allies as new competitors to be kept in check, and the nation's policies toward Asia also went through changes. America extended its open trade policies, even to

Vietnam, and also provided aid to North Korea despite South Korea's protests. This was part of its new strategy to embrace neighbouring countries of China as new allies, thus adding a new sociopolitical dimension to Asia's economy.

America changed its position to curb Asia's exports with various import restrictions, and pressured Asia to open its market. This had the reverse effect of working as a catalyst to integrate Asian nations into an organic unity. In the course of joint reaction to the external pressure, Asians were better able to solidify their interdependency and sense of belonging.[3] What is clearly evident here is that Asian countries, already full of potential for growth, unite more emotionally and systematically when checked, thus amassing even greater energy for growth.

The USA preaches 'fair trade' to its trading partners when in fact, its definition of 'fairness' is highly debatable. The USA demands that its firms be accorded the same treatment as the domestic firms of the countries they are trading with. Furthermore, the USA is attempting to indiscriminately apply its business standards to other countries regardless of regional climate and characteristics. Every country is at a different stage of economic development and has its own set of political and economic issues to consider. By demanding that its standards be applied to other countries wholesale, regardless of regional concerns, the USA violates the very sense of fairness. Even the USA, a country with the most open market in the world, routinely carries out protectionism policies in some sunset industries. Yet, using the strong purchasing power of its market as leverage, it is forcing other countries to adopt its own idea of 'free trade.'

If America, the only superpower, abuses its power to impose arbitrary regulations such as the Super 301, it will end up uniting anti-American forces worldwide. If it keeps pressuring its trading partners, considering as unfair transactions what is disadvantageous to it, the partners, as a way to survive, will enhance their technological competitiveness with the ultimate aim of confronting America. The situation will grow worse as the US administration loses its impartiality and goes on to abuse its power, including applying arbitrary sanctions, listening only to companies that have already lost their international competitiveness. When its automobile market was threatened by low-price Japanese compact cars in the 1970s, America turned to forcing Japan to voluntarily restrict its export volume. This protectionist approach, however, backfired and served as an impetus for Japan to improve the quality and competitiveness of its motor vehicles and finally to concentrate more on exporting luxury cars with higher profit margins. It is important to note that, as a consequence, the US trade deficit with Japan grew even larger.

Whether intentional or not, Pax Americana served as a signal to wake up dormant Asia into developing its economics. Using its mighty power and influence in the international arena, the USA had collected Gulf War expenditures from its allies and even revised international trade rules in its favour. However, in the long run, its military superiority is destined to diminish.

If things are developing in this way, it is also likely that international trade will shrink, finally reducing the economic system merely to self-sufficiency. Those countries with few natural resources and small domestic markets, in particular, will suffer a dramatic shrinkage in income, and thus risk throwing the world into chaos and anarchy. To prevent all this from happening, Asian countries and the rest of the world must speed up open regional integration, which is ultimately aimed at the integration of the world economy.

The truth about the economic development of Asia

There is a school of economic thought that regard the economic development of Asia as a passing phenomenon. It is held that there is little prospect of further economic development in Asia because the Asian model of development was a temporary effect made possible by increased investment of capital and workforce, and not by technological capacity. There is something to that argument. However, what is overlooked is Asia's development energy, the technological potential of its businesses and its workforce, and the synergy created by burden-sharing in the region.

Among the engines of Asia's economic development are its high academic enthusiasm and high-quality and hard-working population, neither of which can be achieved over a short period of time. Its system of bureaucracy is more than 1000 years old, and China and South Korea in particular offer opportunities for even a commoner to rise to a high position through traditional state examinations. Such well-established educational systems provided

South-east Asia with an environment to absorb the technological civilization of the West effectively.

The tradition of respecting academics, combined with Western-style universal schooling, enabled Asia to adopt new technology in a short period of time, and this tradition has been handed down. In Korea, most of the population completes a high school education, and the percentage of those who go on to higher education (50.8 per cent in 1994) is higher than in Germany (35.6 per cent in 1993). Another important factor not to be overlooked is that up to 8 million of those Asians who were educated and living in industrialized nations are going back to their home countries, encouraged by the development of Asia. It was these people who built high-tech industrial complexes in places such as Bangalore, India; Xinzhu, Taiwan; and the Taeduk, Korea, and have internalized and commercialized state-of-the art technology successfully. Software firms in Bangalore are so competitive that they work as subcontractors of world-class corporations such as Microsoft, Intel and Hewlett-Packard.

Table 1.1   The economic situations of major Asian countries

	Population (millions)	GDP ($1 bn)	Exports ($1 bn)	Imports ($1 bn)
South Korea	45	485	125	135
China	1 230	817	155	135
Japan	120	4 964	443	336
Taiwan	22	224	112	104
Hong Kong	6	136	169	160
Singapore	3	57	119	125
Malaysia	19	141	49	47
The Philippines	73	161	13	21
Thailand	60	323	46	52
Indonesia	225	19	41	31
India	930	1 700	18	22
Australia	18	375	50	51
New Zealand	4	52	16	16
Total	2 754	9 454	1 356	1 235

Sources: Dong-A Publishing Co. (1966) *Dong-A Almanac*;
Yunhap Press (1996) *Yunhap Almanac*.

Table 1.2   Average score in TIMSS of six major countries, 1991 (based on 13-year olds)

Country	Average number of school days per year	Maths rank/correct answer rate (%)	Science rank/correct answer rate (%)
China	251	1/80	14/67
South Korea	222	2/73	1/78
Taiwan	222	2/73	2/76
USA	178	15/55	14/67
France	174	7/64	9/69
Switzerland	207	4/71	3/74

Japan, with an excellent-quality workforce, is without a doubt second to none in applying basic technology to product development. Even though the quality of South Korea's higher education lags behind that of advanced countries, its education up to high school is at a world-class level. According to the Test of International Math and Science Studies (TIMSS) conducted by IEA for five years from 1991 on elementary and middle school students from forty-two countries, North-east Asian countries achieved the top ranks, with South Korea competing for first and second places see Table 1.2.

It is not the educational system but student quality, fierce competition for college entrance, and strong academic enthusiasm that allows South Korea to achieve high educational results – despite having more students per class, less investment in education, and substandard facilities. What deserves attention is that the average number of school days per year in South Korea and Taiwan is 222 and in China 251, whereas in the USA the number is just 178 days. In Korea in the past, the rapidly expanding economy resulted in increased demand for college or university graduates. Yet, the relatively small number of colleges and universities could not absorb all the students graduating from high schools and competition to gain admission was intense. Hence, college graduates from respectable institutions automatically had more career opportunities and their paychecks were much higher than those of the high school graduates. While in high school, students study extremely hard to gain admission to colleges and they rank among the best in the world in academic achievement. Yet once in college students are no longer motivated to study and the overall quality of college education lags far behind that of advanced countries. In short, the college education system has the adverse effect of creating mediocre graduates out of once excellent students. The situation is even worse in graduate schools, research institutions and other organizations of higher learning. Also, in business most firms are small or medium-sized and suffer from a serious lack of technological basis and capital. This is a common problem facing a majority of Asian countries and not just limited to Korea.

Since the 1940s, academic enthusiasm has sustained Asia as an engine of economic development despite its backward educational system and environment. Now that such an approach has reached its limit in modern industrial structure, every Asian country is urged to reform its college education practices and thus sharpen its competitive edge. Economic difficulties facing South-east Asian nations in the late 1990s result from their failure to produce highly skilled manpower. Learning a lesson from all this, the whole Asia region should do its utmost to reform education on a long-term basis.

A high savings and investment ratio is another contributing factor to the economic growth of Asia. Most Asian countries save an average of above 30 per cent of GDP, double the ratio of industrialized nations. While savings ratios of the USA, the UK, Germany and France in 1994 were only 16.2 per cent, 13.5 per cent, 21.2 per cent and 19 per cent respectively, those of South Korea and Singapore were up to 35.4 per cent and 38 per cent each. Such a high savings ratio is a product of Asian history – for most Asians in the past, saving was the only way to buy houses or durable consumer goods, since their income was unstable and consumer finance was underdeveloped. Also, frugality became a part of life for those who had gone through poverty, and those who were too busy working to survive had no time to spend. The burden of preparing for job loss, retirement or war fell on them because of political and economic instability. A high savings ratio had the dual effect of providing an investment source for economic development and stabilizing prices by discouraging consumption.

A 'dedicated work ethic' is one of the most important factors for the robust growth of Asian economies. In agricultural societies like Asia, hard work is a prerequisite for a good harvest. In countries with an agriculture-unfriendly environment, including South Korea in particular, people had to work extremely hard while they could

Table 1.3   Ratios of savings and investments as a share of GDP, 1996

Country	Savings ratio as a share of GDP	Investment ratio as a share of GDP
Japan	31.4	28.9
South Korea	35.4	36.2
Taiwan	30.8	33.8
Singapore	32.2	38.0
Thailand*	35.9	40.1
Indonesia*	30.5	34.3
Malaysia*	38.1	38.5
China*	40.2	41.2
The Philippines*	15.6	24.0
USA	16.2	17.1
UK	13.5	15.4
Germany	21.2	24.5
France	19.0	18.0
India*	23.8	23.2
New Zealand	20.4	22.3

Notes: * Denotes statistics for 1993.
Source: Bank of Korea, 'Korean Economy in the World Bureau of Statistics', *International Statistics Quarterly*, International Monetary Fund.

in order to survive and not starve. This tradition of a dedicated work ethic passed into the manufacturing industries, therefore producing a high-quality labour force. Working hours per week were up to 37.8 and 49.2, for Japan and South Korea respectively, leaving the people with little time for consumption, an additional advantage of hard work. In recent decades, however, flooded with Western-style consumption culture that they came in contact with through their rapid industrialization, economic growth and informationalization, Asian countries have gone through dramatic changes in many ways, such as loss of the 'hungry spirit' that made their economic development possible; sharp decreases in working hours and days; and changed views on labour among others. A Korean saying that a person's riches is rarely handed down to the third generation is coming true. This is the first and foremost lesson that Asian countries, including South Korea, should learn, since there is a high possibility that the future of Asia will be overshadowed by the loss of willingness to work with the increase of income and the advent of a generation that has no idea of what poverty is like.

Table 1.4   Average working hours per week in manufacturing industries

S. Korea	Hong Kong	India*	Japan	The Philippines**	Singapore	Taiwan	Thailand
49.2	43.8	46.5	37.8	45.5	49.3	46.4	49.5

Notes: * Record for 1992; ** Record for 1994.
Source: Bureau of Statistics of Korea (1997) *International Statistics Almanac.*

Though they surfaced with the free fall of the Thailand baht in July 1997, problems among Asian economies had already been predicted to some extent, being side-effects of the rapid growth that manifested itself when the economic bubble burst. The excessive depreciation of the Japanese yen and Chinese yuan is generally considered to be the main factor contributing to the rapid fall of the competitiveness of South-east Asian countries. A more fundamental reason behind this, however, is lax economic management and a weakened spirit of frugality. When discussing the rapid reduction of the Korean economy since 1988, a common criticism levelled at Koreans is that 'they uncorked the Champagne bottle too early' – an expression applicable also to the rest of the Asian countries.

Humans naturally seek to fulfil higher-level desires after their primary desire for survival is met to some extent. Each government in Asian countries should therefore pay attention to make sure that their people foster sound and future-orientated thinking and a strong work ethic so as not to lose their creativeness and willingness to work.

Light and darkness of Asian economies

Asian economies have many problems. South Korea, for example, achieved its high-level growth by mobilizing powerful export-driven growth policies, especially in the simple processing industries based on low-wage labour. Now having had a dramatic increase in wages, South Korea is not only closely pursued by emerging economies but is also kept in check by industrialized nations. Even though it is urgent for South Korea to continue to restructure its economy into a technology-intensive one in order to overcome this difficulty, it is handicapped by insufficient technological capacity and infrastructure. This is a problem also faced by other Asian nations. In the case of infrastructure, the gestation period of capital is long and the investment profit ratio low, while the market interest rate is relatively high, barring large-scale investment in infrastructure. This results in a bottleneck of development.[4]

South Korea, just like other Asian nations, did not have any problems with logistics costs during the 1960s, the initial stage of economic development, but in the 1990s this cost takes up 17 per cent of manufacturing costs, about double that of the USA and Japan –

which, seriously harms its national competitiveness. Traffic conges-
tion in Bangkok is already out of control and situations in other
Asian developing countries are no better. Without a dramatic
expansion of the infrastructure, the export competitiveness of Asia
will weaken significantly in the future.

A single question that draws the attention of the world is 'Will
East Asia be able to continue with the high-level growth achieved
since the 1950s, and can that kind of growth be replicated in the
Third World?' One note of caution: for Asian-style economic development to be more than just a passing phenomenon made possible
only by simple capital investment and an increase in low-wage
labour, it is imperative to boost productivity through continuous
technological development. In fact, Asian-style growth was successful mainly because of large-scale investment and increased employment. Such growth naturally reaches its end when its quantitative
expansion stagnates. Therefore, to overcome this, Asian countries
must upgrade their workforce and internalize technical strengths.
The 'dictatorship-for-development' characteristic of some Asian
countries has a tendency to lose momentum once some degree of
growth has been achieved. This is because, as the level of incomes
goes up, political demands erupt among the populace, entrepreneurs lose their entrepreneurial sprit because of unreasonable
systems, and workers lose their willingness to work.

In the late 1990s the Korean economy has been experiencing
extreme difficulties. Detrimental factors such as the government's
non-transparent management of the economy; the collusion of politics and economics; the underdeveloped finance system; and indis-
creet borrowing by the Chaebol (conglomerates) have combined
with the financial crisis in South-east Asia to pull down South
Korea's economy. However, with the financial aid of the
International Monetary Fund (IMF), the people, businesses and government of South Korea are once again uniting to restore the
country to its former glory, and casting a favourable light on its
future. Additionally, the recent peaceful transfer of power between
the ruling party and the opposition has signified South Korea's
political maturation and will be a contributing factor to the
country's future democratic development.

With its remarkable economic growth aptly dubbed 'the Miracle
of the Han River', South Korea once served as a model of economic

development for many developing countries. If South Korea is able to navigate the current crisis, it will once again become a model of economic development to be emulated. But the fate of the Asian economies will largely depend on how South Korea's economy develops in the near future.

Notes

1. Among the investment of overseas capital in China from 1979 to 1991, overseas Chinese in Hong Kong, Taiwan and so on provided 66.7 per cent. Mitsubishi Research Institute (1996) *Total Forecasting of Asia*.
2. The total value added produced by overseas Chinese is estimated at US$5 trillion; and the total assets, US$2 billion, two-thirds of those of Japan. Ibid., p. 91.
3. Representative examples include ASEAN, East Asian Economic Group (EAEG), South Asian Association for Regional Co-operation (SAARC) and so on.
4. Asian countries try to attract foreign capital to their infrastructure sector by utilizing the BOT (Build, Operate, Transfer) method. In particular, Indonesia pushed for privatization by allowing up to 95 per cent of foreign investment.

2
The Motive Power for World Economic Integration

By utilizing the low labour costs and production base in Asia, the USA has successfully stabilized prices in its domestic market and advanced its industries since the Second World War. Caught completely off guard by the rapid development of Asia's productivity and technological know-how, the USA struggled to implement measures to keep the region's growth in check. Ironically, this move by the USA brought Asian countries closer together and further helped to strengthen their solidarity. Japan moved its production facilities to developing countries in order to avoid import regulations and realize lower production costs. If there were wage increases in one country, Japan would withdraw its production facilities from that country and move to another. As this process repeated itself throughout the region, developing countries in Asia, one after another, were able to increase their range of technology and realize their potential for development. As a result, new demands were created and intraregional trade dependency increased, securing Asia's position in the international arena.

As shown in Tables 2.1 and Table 2.2, the intraregional trade dependency of fourteen Asian nations increased from 30.9 per cent in 1960 to 51.2 per cent in 1995 – which proves that the economic interdependency among countries within the region is gradually rising. Developmental stages and economic conditions differ in each country, but nevertheless, the internal environment for co-operation is becoming favourable – for example, incentives for intraregionally transacted products such as a tariff exemption.

Table 2.1 Intraregional trade matrix of Asian nations, 1960 (US$ millions)

	South Korea	Japan	China	Taiwan	Hong Kong	Singapore	The Philippines	Malaysia	Thailand	Indonesia	Australia	New Zealand	India	Vietnam	Asia (c)	Other	Total Exports (D)	C/D (%)
South Korea		20			3										23	9	32	71.9
Japan	100		3	102	156	87	156	32	118	110	144	12	109	62	1 190	2 865	4 055	29.3
China	6	21			278	46	2	5	4	57	11	6	7	3	447	1 442	1 889	23.7
Taiwan		78			21	4	2						2		107	58	165	64.8
Hong Kong	6	21	46			22	8	10	58	29	21	17	2	3	249	495	744	33.5
Singapore	8	90	21	15	15		20	206	18	32	44	3	23	14	578	558	1 136	50.9
The Philippines	9	75	2	2	8	20		19	8	1	1		1		146	388	534	27.3
Malaysia	1	72	5		10	206	19		25	9	19		27		393	563	956	41.1
Thailand		15	2		58	58	8	77		10	1		2	5	236	167	403	58.6
Indonesia		62	57		29	194	1	9	10		32		6		400	440	840	47.6
Australia	7	313	12		21	44	1	19	1	30		133	37		618	1 443	2 061	30.0
New Zealand		29									30		3		62	785	847	7.3
India		61	7		2	23	1	27	2	6	46	17		2	194	1 139	1 333	14.6
Vietnam															24	62	86	28.0
Asia (c)	137	962	127	130	567	626	216	575	200	284	349	188	217	89	4 667	10 414	15 081	30.9
Other	150	3 530	169	1 634	511	706	347	126	243	290	2 013	596	1 907	151	12 373	104 038	116 411	10.6
Total Imports (D)	287	4 492	296	1 764	1 078	1 332	563	701	443	574	2 362	784	2 124	240	17 040	114 452	131 492	13.0
C/D (%)	47.2	21.4	42.9	7.4	52.6	47.0	38.4	82.0	45.1	49.5	14.8	24.0	10.2	37.1	27.4	9.1	11.5	

Source: International Monetary Fund (1961) *Directory of Trade Statistics.*

Table 2.2 Intraregional trade matrix of Asian nations, 1996 (US$ billions)

	South Korea	Japan	China	Taiwan	Hong Kong	Singapore	The Philippines	Malaysia	Thailand	Indonesia	Australia	New Zealand	India	Vietnam	Asia (c)	Other	Total Exports (D)	C/D (%)
South Korea		16.0	11.5	4.0	11.2	6.5	1.9	4.3	2.7	3.2	1.8	0.2	1.9	1.6	65.9	64.6	130.5	50.5
Japan	29.4		21.8	25.9	25.4	20.8	8.4	15.3	18.3	9.1	7.4	1.7	2.4	1.1	187.5	223.7	411.2	45.6
China	7.5	30.9		2.8	32.9	3.8	1.0	1.4	1.3	1.4	1.7	0.2	0.7	0.8	86.5	64.6	151.5	57.2
Taiwan	2.7	14.9	16.2		15.9	5.3	1.6	3.9	3.1	2.2	1.9	0.4	0.5	1.3	70.2	45.5	115.7	60.7
Hong Kong	2.9	11.8	61.9	4.3		4.9	2.1	1.7	1.8	1.0	2.5	0.3	0.8	0.6	96.7	83.8	180.5	53.6
Singapore	3.8	10.3	3.4	4.9			2.3	22.5	7.1	1.0	2.9	0.4	2.1	1.7	72.5	52.6	125.1	58.0
The Philippines	0.4	3.7	0.3	0.7	0.9	1.2		0.7	0.8	0.1	0.4	0.02	0.2	0.1	9.2	11.3	20.5	44.9
Malaysia	2.4	10.5	1.9	3.2	4.6	16.0	0.9		3.2	1.2	1.2	0.2	1.2	0.3	46.9	31.3	78.2	60.2
Thailand	1.0	9.4	1.9	1.4	3.2	6.7	0.6	2.0		0.8	0.8	0.1	0.2	0.5	28.6	27.2	55.8	51.3
Indonesia	3.6	13.8	2.1	1.7	1.5	2.7	0.6	1.1	0.9		1.3	0.1	0.4	0.2	30.0	18.1	48.1	62.4
Australia	5.7	12.0	3.0	2.7	2.3	2.3	0.7	1.7	1.3	2.4		4.3	0.9	0.2	39.6	21.4	61.0	64.9
New Zealand	0.7	2.2	0.4	0.4	0.5	0.2	0.2	0.3	0.2	0.2			0.08	0.04	8.4	5.9	14.3	58.7
India	0.8	2.5	0.7	0.4	1.8	0.8	0.7	0.5	0.6	0.6	0.4	0.01		0.1	10.0	24.4	34.4	29.1
Vietnam	1.8	0.3	0.3	0.2	0.4	0.2	0.2	0.1	0.06	0.1	0.3	0.01	0.02		3.8	3.1	6.9	55.1
Asia (c)	60.9	139.9	125.7	52.8	111.5	71.8	21.3	55.5	41.4	22.3	25.4	8.0	10.8	8.5	755.8	677.5	1 433.3	52.7
Other	89.5	209.6	13.1	60.2	87.1	59.7	10.5	22.5	32.1	20.7	36.1	6.7	29.2	5.2	682.2	3 153.5	3 835.7	17.7
Total Imports (D)	150.4	349.5	138.8	113.0	198.6	131.5	31.8	78.0	73.5	43.0	61.5	14.7	40	13.7	1 438	3 831	5 269	27.3
C/D (%)	40.5	40.0	90.6	46.7	56.1	54.6	67.0	71.2	56.3	51.9	41.3	54.5	37.0	62.0	52.6	17.7	27.2	

Source: International Monetary Fund (1997) Directory of Trade Statistics.

According to a survey by the Economist Intelligence Unit (EIU), Asia's market share in the world was 37 per cent (excluding Australia) in 1995, leaving North America (20.5 per cent) and Western Europe (20.5 per cent) far behind. This was made possible by Asia's internal trade, which had increased 154-fold, while global trade increased only 38-fold, since the 1960s.

The vision and role of Asia

World economies at the time of writing are developing in contradictory ways, both globalizing and localizing at the same time. In the late 1990s, tens of regional economic treaties are being conceived and realized world-wide. The common goals of these treaties include internal tariff reduction, common external tariffs, and the free circulation of capital and labour. *The European Union (EU)* aims ultimately at complete internal integration, while North American Free Trade Agreement (NAFTA) pursues internal trade liberalization only. However, both are characterized by their exclusion of non-members.

To keep abreast of current global economic trends, Asian countries should not only enhance their technological capacity and competitiveness but also form a common regional market based on open regionalism which embraces any nation that agrees to the principle of economic integration, regardless of its location. In this vein, such a common market should be World Free Trade Area (WOFTA), an embodiment of World Trade Organization (WTO) spirit, rather than East Asian Economic Group (EAEG) or Asian Free Trade Area (AFTA).

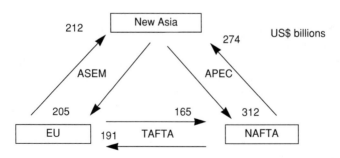

Figure 2.1   The world's three economic blocs and expected trade volume between them
Source: International Monetary Fund (1997) *Directory of Trade Statistics.*

Table 2.3   The world's three economic blocs

	EU	New Asia	North America
Total GDP (US$ billions)	8 554	9 454	8 632
Total population (millions)	370	2 754	380
Per capita GDP (US$)	23 319	3 432	22 716
Economic growth rate (1990–2000)	2.5%	7%	3%

Note: GDP of North America is the record for 1995.
Source: Korea Trade Investment Promotion Agency, inside data.

In the future, the Asian region (including India) with its 28 billion people, will form the largest economic bloc and along with the NAFTA and the EU, will constitute the three major economic blocs in the world. Member nations will be the traditional East Asian nations and new ones such as Australia, New Zealand and India. Also, in addition to the aforementioned countries, there is a good possibility that far-eastern Russia, because of its increasing economic dependence on the geographical proximity to Asia, will be included in the New Asian economic bloc. In the early twenty first century, the Asian bloc will account for more than half of the world economy based on its huge population and annual real growth rate of 7 per cent.

Some people are understandably sceptical about the possibility of realizing this New Asian economic bloc. They cite the first reason as being an insufficient sense of collectivity in the bloc. They argue that gaps in the economy among member nations are wider compared to the EU or the NAFTA, and there are a variety of nations and cultures as well. Nevertheless, the members have psychological homogeneity since they share a history of oppression by the West. They also share an aspiration for economic development because all have experienced abject poverty. Once institutionally bound in a systematic way, these countries would be able to utilize their diversities, at present thought of as a weakness, to form an interdependent economic structure – thus creating a stronger synergy.

One thing to be extremely cautious of in constituting an Asian economic bloc is exclusionism. The EU and the NAFTA are exclusive, but the Asian economic bloc must uphold the open-door principle. In the historical trend of global economic integration, Asia is no doubt a mediator between the wealthy nations and those in absolute poverty in that it has achieved economic growth after overcoming moments of ordeal throughout history. In this respect, for the sake of procedural convenience, there is a need to form a bloc with North-east Asian and ASEAN countries, India and Australia as starting members, and afterwards gradually to embrace all the countries that share the spirit of economic integration, including Muslim countries and Russia. The name, therefore should be WOFTA (World Free Trade Area) rather than AFTA (Asian Free Trade Area).

Another point of caution is conflict among nations over hegemony of the bloc. Every nation is naturally in a different stage of development. Advanced countries should encourage latecomers and continue to develop in conjunction with the newcomers rather than exploit them. There are concerns that what the USA seems to be doing is revealing its intention not to lose its grip on the hegemony of the world economy. Even though the USA is leading the NAFTA, it is a member of two other economic blocs at the same time – Asia – Pacific Economic Cooperation (APEC) with the Asian nations, and Trans Atlantic Free Trade Agreement (TAFTA) with EU member nations. It is very regrettable that the USA seems to be busy deterring the formation of any group that precludes its participation rather than working to achieve economic integration through mutual co-operation and elimination of exclusionism between the economic blocs.

Economic development and the role of government

The rise and fall of a country has something in common with that of an individual. Just like a human being, a country that has invested more effort than another and developed a unique formula for success achieves a dramatic outcome. But when the nation's energy is depleted, the economy also declines. In the book *The Rise and Fall of the Great Powers*,[1] Paul Kennedy wrote that a new superpower is built during the synergy process of its defence and economic power, but superpower so constituted is destined to collapse when its economy is laden down with an excessive defence burden. The USSR flourished for around seventy-five years as a strong and powerful nation before withering. In the process, the rest of the world learned an important lesson – that inefficiency and excessive military spending by a despotic state are the stumbling blocks for a country in pursuing technology-based development.

On the other hand, several measures China took following the establishment of diplomatic relations with the USA were very appropriate. By dissolving collective farms and recognizing individual land ownership, China achieved remarkable growth in agricultural productivity and as a result, took a giant step towards solving the problem of its chronic food shortages. Also, the country was able to cut its military spending through efficient arms reduction and by adopting a uniquely Chinese system in which each army crops procured revenue resources by managing its own businesses. This paved the way for the military to take part in the country's economic development. Internationally, China attracted foreign capital and technology by aggressively promoting its cheap labour and the huge potential of its market. Also, in an effort to improve productivity, the country is privatizing many state-owned enterprises that have for a long time been the very symbol of inefficiency. As a result of these measures, Chinese products currently account for a lion's share in the mid to low-technology goods market and the country is steadily expanding into high-tech products as well.

Economic growth is the end product achieved when the diverse energies of a nation are combined, and not by the efforts of businesses alone. In a society where entrepreneurs are regarded merely as 'those who are frantically after money', they are apt to lose their entrepreneurial drive as well as their creativity. Entrepreneurs were treated as national heroes when Britain flourished and they were at the centre of the ruling power when Venice was growing into a world-class empire, but when they were denounced as 'social enemies', their nations foundered at the same time.

Were it not for wholehearted national and governmental support of entrepreneurs, Asia could not have accomplished its concentrated economic growth since the 1950s. Such support may have stemmed from the people's desire to identify with successful entrepreneurs. Paradoxically, the collusion of business and politics is a necessity for both the businesses and the state to make inroads into the global market. A nation that combines its national energies in order to explore overseas markets can create a miracle. On the contrary, when formed for the purpose of giving favours to certain people, business – politics collusion ends up being a hotbed of corruption, and encouraging extreme inefficiency.

The role of government in Asian economic development is like a double-edged sword. Asia owes much of its prosperity in the 1990s to the roles of government. In the initial stages of economic development, any business entity is likely to suffer from a lack of capital and technology. Asian governments were able to secure at least a limited amount of capital and also maximize their growth rate by concentrating their support on export priority industries. Governments led economic development by actively promoting export businesses with various incentives such as tax exemptions, subsidies, long-term and low-interest-rate policy loans, and investment in infrastructure.

In the process of government-led development, however, these measures of support were inevitably accompanied by corruption among government employees. Under a powerful administrative system, those who work for the government are underpaid and given too much power, creating a strong possibility for a collusive link with the business sector. Corruption greatly undermined economic efficiency. In the past, Asia could maximize its export competitiveness simply with capital investment and tax benefits, since its economies had developed while being centred on labour-intensive light industries. Now Asian countries can no longer continue the past practices as production costs go up and export goods are changing. The launch of the WTO effectively ended various kinds of government support, including subsidies, which came to be regarded as unfair trade practices.

To cope with such difficult situation, Asia needs to restructure its industries by boosting productivity and developing high value-added priority export goods. In reality, however, Asia is not fully capable of developing technology on its own and is also experiencing difficulties in purchasing technology, because industrialized nations tightly control its transfer, and the rise in logistics costs resulting from a lack of infrastructure is hampering profitability. Also, the ratio of wage increases surpasses that of productivity since workers' expectancy goes up with sustained high growth – thus discouraging entrepreneurial drive. Furthermore, industrialized nations are increasing pressure to force emerging economies to open their markets. With all these factors combined, the newly industrialized economies are finding themselves in a deep quagmire.

Of course, even without pressure from the advanced nations, Asia should open its markets in order to boost export competitiveness, stabilize prices and meet consumer demands. The rules of competition should be applied impartially – but the sudden and indiscriminate opening of domestic markets will result in damage, even to future industries that do not yet have an established base. The government must therefore assume the role of controlling the speed of opening based on a long-term perspective. Governments should reduce their size through bold administrative reform, and privatize inefficient state-owned companies and unnecessary government departments in order to reduce financial deficits and enhance productivity.

New Zealand cut the number of central government employees drastically from 85 000 to 40 000, and the number of local government employees from 180 000 to 38 000 and privatized the Ministry of Communications.[2] As a consequence, the communications sector recorded a 20 per cent cost reduction and an 85 per cent productivity improvement, and the railway bureau, despite a 50 per cent

Table 2.4   Numbers of personnel cut in central government offices, New Zealand

Department	1985	1994
Ministry of Transportation	4 358	57
Ministry of Scientific Research	2 418	34
Ministry of Forestry	7 796	133
Ministry of Health	3 933	394
Ministry of Administration	827	144
Ministry of Education	2 053	639
Ministry of Agriculture and Fisheries	5 928	3 010
Ministry of Domestic Affairs	3 326	2 762
Customs Office	1 213	826
Ministry of Finance	489	387
Ministry of Labour	2 370	1 967
Office of National Tax Administration	4 150	5 079
Office of Premier	55	118
Other	43 169	23 808
Total	85 378	40 158

Source: Yi, Kye-Sik and Moon, Hyeong-Pyo (1996) *Government Reform*, Korea Development Institute.

reduction in the cargo fare, went into the black. For harbours in particular, waiting time and harbour charges dropped by 56 per cent and 50 per cent respectively, despite the 50 per cent decrease in the number of workers. The above mentioned trend is found not only in New Zealand but also in all the industrialized nations including the UK,[3] the USA, Canada and Japan. Therefore a revolutionary paradigm shift and a bold action plan on a supernational basis are necessary for New Asian nations if they wish to continue their high-level growth.

Economic development and democracy

What enabled most Asian nations to restrict personal freedom for the sake of economic development was the people's dire state: that is, their predicament and starvation drove them to tolerate even dictatorship in exchange for enough food. However, it is human nature to have higher aspirations, such as self-realization and a search for meaning of life once the basic need for food is met. In the case of South Korea, popular demands for democratization from the late 1980s led to tremendous sacrifices before finally producing the civilian government of the 1990s. South Korea's economic status improved dramatically as its per capita income passed the US$10 000 mark and led to the country's entry into the Organization for Economic Co-operation and Development (OECD). While the country still has various problems to solve, it has effectively laid the foundations for more democratization in the future.

While being successful economically, Singapore and Taiwan have a long way to go before achieving political maturity, and Indonesia is in a similar political situation despite its economic success and huge potential stemming from its abundant natural resources and population of 190 million. Land comprising thousands of islands and a diverse population may have enabled the country to sustain its existing political system, but the situation will be different in the post-Suharto Indonesia. Most Asian nations can be expected to endure hardship for a considerable amount of time in the democratization process. Only a country that successfully navigates this process will obtain advanced nation status and sustain self-growth.

The dynamics and features of Asian economic growth

In *The East Asian Miracle*,[4] published in 1993, the World Bank characterizes Asian economic growth as follows.

Continuous high growth

The eight High-Performing Asian Economies (HPAE) have recorded a real income growth rate of 5.5 per cent annually since 1960, while China has recorded 5.8 per cent since 1965. The percentages are higher than those of any other economic bloc worldwide – and are a distinguishing feature of East Asian economies. In particular, the growth of North-east Asian countries and Singapore stand out.

Narrowing of the income gap and the elimination of abject poverty

Narrowing the income gap is a task as difficult as developing an economy, since it is intricately intertwined with individual interests and can ignite various kinds of social problems. Despite this, East Asian countries, with the exception of Malaysia, have realized relatively equal distribution of income and opportunities since the beginning of their development, which is all the more surprising considering their high GDP growth rate. In effect, they are meeting the two goals of growth and equality simultaneously.

South Korea is the most outstanding in distribution of wealth, and Thailand is the least notable.

Industrial restructuring and improvement of agricultural productivity

The continuation of economic development tends to bring down gradually the share of agriculture in total industries – a phenomenon found in the development process across the globe, and East Asian countries are very swift in such industrial restructuring. As shown in Table 2.5, the share of agriculture in GDP and the agricultural population are declining, yet the volume of agricultural products and productivity improvement remain at all-time highs. Such productivity improvement is mainly attributable to investment in infrastructure (mostly in former Japanese colonies); farmland rearrangement (South Korea and Taiwan); farming mechanization; plant breeding; and

Table 2.5   Shares of agricultural population and agriculture in GDP

Country	Share of agricultural population (%) 1995	Share of agriculture in GDP (%) 1993
South Korea	13.5	7.0
China	71.3	19.0
Hong Kong	0.8	0
India	61.6	31.0
Indonesia	53.2	19.0
Japan	5.5	2.0
Malaysia	22.9	16.0
The Philippines	42.4	22.0
Singapore	0.2	0
Taiwan	10.4	4.0
Vietnam	69.3	n/a
Australia	4.5	3.0
New Zealand	10.1	8.0

Note: Share of agricultural population = those engaged in agriculture/economically active population × 100.
Source: Bureau of Statistics of Korea (1997) *International Statistics Almanac*.

improvement of the soil. Taiwan, in particular, showed a 45 per cent growth in the agricultural sector in the 1950s with the help of a government development programme. This growth resulted mainly from the boost in agricultural productivity.

Since the late 1960s, while the rest of the world has devastated the agricultural sector by funnelling funds collected from this sector to other industries under various tax schemes and food-price adjustment policies, the Asian nations have fostered agriculture by implementing measures such as reductions in related taxes.

High export growth rate

The most notable feature of East Asia is its high export growth rate. Its share in global export volume skyrocketed from 8 per cent in 1965 to 25 per cent 1996. Japan has maintained its position as the world's biggest exporter of industrial products since 1965 and at the time of writing its share of the international market is 12 per cent. Furthermore, exports of industrial products

Table 2.6   Share in exports of East Asian economies

Economic group	Share in global export volume			
	1965	*1980*	*1990*	*1996*
Total Export Volume				
Japan	5.0	7.0	9.0	7.6
Four Dragons[a]	1.5	3.8	6.7	10.2
SouthEast Asian NIES[b]	1.5	2.2	2.4	3.3
HPAE[c]	7.9	13.1	18.2	21.1
Export Volume of Industrial Products				
Japan	7.8	11.6	11.8	8.0*
Four Dragons[a]	1.5	5.3	7.9	10.1*
SouthEast Asian NIES[b]	0.1	0.4	1.5	3.8*
HPAE[c]	9.4	17.3	21.3	21.8*

Notes: [a] South Korea, Hong Kong, Taiwan, Singapore.
[b] Indonesia, Malaysia, Thailand.
[c] Japan + a + b.
* Figures for 1994.
Sources: International Monetary Fund (1997) *Directory of Trade Statistics*; Bureau of Statistics (1997) *Major Economic Indicators of Korea.*

from South Korea, Taiwan, Hong Kong and Singapore grew at a rate four times greater than that of Japan during the 1970s and 1980s.

Rapid structural change in population

The phenomenon where population growth rate stagnates because of a decline in birth and mortality rates began to emerge in Europe and the USA during the period of the Industrial Revolution, and such a change in population structure is now taking place with great speed in East Asian nations. In the 1960s these countries maintained a high population growth rate through a high birth rate and widespread health benefits. In the case of South Korea, the population growth rate shrank from 2.6 per cent during 1960–70, to 1.1 per cent during 1980–90; from 2.5 per cent to 1.4 per cent in Hong Kong; and from 3.8 per cent to 1.8 per cent in Thailand. In East Asia, only a generation ago, the population structure resembled an hourglass – that is, the infant and elderly populations were larger than that of the youth. However, it is swiftly changing into a 'pot' type, where the working age group of 25–59-year-olds accounts for a larger proportion of the population. This change, which took over a century in Europe, has been accomplished in only a generation in East Asia.

High growth rate of savings and large-scale investment

Most economists have agreed that investment is the most crucial factor in economic development. In closed economies, savings deposits equal the amount of investment, while open economies have foreign loans and savings. The domestic savings ratio determines the rate of investment. Asia's savings ratio, which had lagged behind South Americas in 1965, exceeded it by 20 per cent in 1990.

Asia's savings ratio remained low because of the large number of dependent members in families. With the structural changes in the population as the infant and elderly populations decreased, saving rate increases among the working-age population resulted in the brisk entry of a new workforce into the market. Such changes are an important factor in economic development. In 1965, Asia's investment ratio was at a level similar to that of South America, but almost doubled it by 1990.

The upgrading of effective human resources

East Asian nations have traditionally had highly-educated, good-quality human resources. Well before the beginning of economic development, most Asian countries had implemented universal schooling for elementary education. Secondary education in Asia also proved superior to that of other developing country groups. In South Korea, more than 98.7 per cent went on to secondary school in 1996. In most Asian countries, the disparity in educational opportunities between men and women is decreasing with great speed.

The rapid enhancement of productivity

Productivity enhancement is one of the most conspicuous characteristics and also the very core element of economic development, since GDP growth basically depends on labour productivity improvement of workers. Three factors boost labour productivity: first, increases in material capital; second, a highly-educated workforce; and third, qualitative elements such as a capacity for technological development and organization, specialization and innovation in the workplace.

Viewed from this perspective, the remarkable economic growth of Asia resulted mainly from the rapid accumulation of material and human capital. In most cases, a 10 per cent increase of investment rate to GDP leads to an 0.5 per cent increase in per capita GDP growth rate, and when an additional 10 per cent of elementary or secondary students continue their studies at a higher level, per capita income goes up by 0.3 per cent. Even the relatively outdated technology of industrialized nations can bring about technological reform in developing countries, and such technology can be transferred cheaply when machines are introduced, thus dramatically improving productivity. Nevertheless, for further growth, continuous productivity enhancement as well as investment in material and human capital are required.

Prospects for Asian economies and their roles

While it is true that Asian nations have achieved their considerable success by emulating Japan's high-level growth policies, they have also experienced similar side-effects. Just as Japan suffered severely when its bubble economy burst, so South-east Asian nations are experiencing similar hardships.

Asia, after some ups and downs will in the foreseeable future solidify a sense of belonging and commonness, thereby rapidly intensifying the region's economic interdependency. In effect, Asia will take the lead in a triangular structure where the EU is connected with Asia Europe Meeting (ASEM), and NAFTA is connected with APEC. At the same time, Asia should do its utmost to transfer to underdeveloped countries the experience it has gained from a history of overcoming oppression and subsistence economy. In this manner it can help develop global economies and correct the imbalance in economic prosperities. First of all, every Asian nation should make a strenuous effort to develop a spiritual energy that can sustain high growth, and invest aggressively in education. Without such effort, there will be neither technological development nor the willingness to work, leaving Asia without the energy it sorely needs to enter the new stage of qualitative growth.

New Asia, the world's biggest economic bloc, will lead global economic growth in conjunction with the EU and the NAFTA, among others. By contributing to global economic integration and prosperity, the emergence of New Asia will be the most realistic alternative for the global economy that might fall into confusion with the rise of 'Pax Americana'.

Notes

1. Kennedy, Paul M., (1989) *The Rise and Fall of the Great Powers: Economic Change and Military Conflict from 1500 to 2000.* (Vintage)
2. Particularly in the public sector, the number decreased by approximately 20 per cent from 347 000 in 1985 to 280 000 in 1994. Yi, Kye-Sik and Moon, Hyeong-Pyo (1996,) Korean Development Institute
3. In the case of the UK, the number of employees in the central and regional governments and other areas of the public sector decreased by 25 per cent from 6.55 million in 1980 to 4.91 million in 1992. In 1993 in particular, annual government funds dropped to £500 million from £3 billion in 1979 and this played a major part in constructively balancing public finances.
4. Oxford University Press (1993) *The East Asian Miracle.*

Part II
Individual Countries

3
Japan: The Fuse for Asian Economic Development

The long, narrow Japanese archipelago lies north to south, resembling a curved breakwater for the vast Eurasian continent. Yet this seemingly insignificant archipelago is home to the world's second largest economic powerhouse. Up to the 1850s, two centuries after its first contact with Europeans, Japan was no more than a Far Eastern hermit to European eyes. That is why many tend to believe that Japan emerged as a modern industrialized nation overnight with the Meiji Restoration, which is a totally erroneous point of view.

Japan took a huge leap forward with regard to its politics, culture and economy, going through two great 'awakenings' in its history. The first was initiated by Koguryō and Packjae, dynasties of Korea that escaped from the unification of the Korean peninsula by Shilla in the seventh century; the second by Western civilization in the nineteenth century. It is not an exaggeration to say that the Japanese were second to none in admiring and learning from Western civilization. This attitude of the Japanese people is also reflected in their language: 17 per cent of modern Japanese vocabulary is borrowed. While harmoniously accepting the two contrasting civilizations of China and the West, Japan has added its own flavour to the strong points of each culture, thus creating a culture unique to the country. Therefore, to have a correct view of Japanese economic development, one must first become familiar with the history of the country that has been producing this marvellous growth energy.

Three drivers of reunification

It is the era of Tokugawa that is the most significant in Japanese history, both politically and economically. Japan enjoyed peace for the 285 years of the Tokugawa era before the Meiji Restoration, as the ruling system that had been in a chaotic state after the fall of Kamakura Bakuhoo was stabilized. During this important era, the foundations were laid for the promotion of its national wealth. It was also a period when the archipelago's unification process, begun by Oda Nobunaka (1534–82) was continued by Tokugawa Ieyasu and subsequently completed by Toyotomi Hideyoshi (1536–98).

Oda mobilized up to 3000 riflemen and by gaining the upper hand subdued the Japanese archipelago, which had been divided. He completely changed the face of war by mass-producing duplicates of the muskets purchased from the Portuguese, marking the first 'Gunpowder Revolution' in Asia. The musket called 'Tanekashima' was a formidable new weapon to the daimyō[1] who had only known conventional weapons. Despite his efforts Oda was betrayed and killed by one of his men, Akechi Mitsuhide, before the unification of Japan was achieved. After his death, Toyotomi, who had been his right-hand man, succeeded him and completed the reunification. Encouraged by the unification, Toyotomi went on to pursue his ambition to conquer Chosun, but was defeated. His invasion of the Korean peninsula inflicted terrible damage on both sides and was the eventual cause of his death in 1598.

The third unifier of the archipelago was Tokugawa Ieyasu (1542–1616), the strongest daimyō. He seized control of Japan in a sweeping victory in the great battle of Sekigahara in 1600. He stormed Osaka castle in 1614 and massacred Toyotomi's descendants before rearranging the nation into 250 daimyō-controlled units. Twenty-three Shinpan, kinsfolk of Tokugawa, were allocated fiefs totalling 2 600 000 gokus.[2] To 130 Hudai daimyō, who had been serving him before the Sekigahara battle, territories of 6 700 000 gokus in total were distributed. Territories that total 9 800 000 gokus were given to ninety-seven Tojama daimyō, the large-scale daimyō who became followers of Tokugawa after the Sekigahara battle, or who chose not to confront him despite hostile relations with him before the battle.

The Tokugawa Bakuhoo for the first time had an accurate estimate of 25 900 000 gokus across the nation, including the total feudal

45

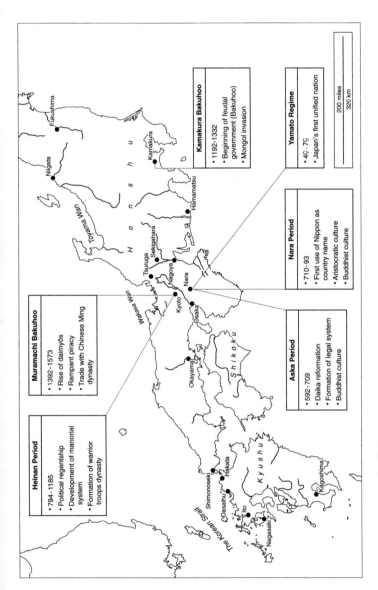

Map 3.1   Japan in the Tokugawa era

estates of 19 100 000 gokus and some 6 800 000 gokus of Bakuhoo owned Tenryo. The Bakuhoo paved the way for modern Japan in all aspects. Even though it prohibited the inflow of foreign culture by upholding seclusionism, and devised pre-modern systems and laws, the Bakuhoo political structure was the most efficient system of rule for continuing stable growth under the circumstances of the time.

In an island country like Japan, with rugged mountainous terrain, a threat from outside is rarely encountered. Since the population did not feel the need for a strong centralist system, the Bakuhoo had no other choice but to compromise with the existing powers. The grand task of unification was carried out by Oda, Toyotomi, and Tokugawa, and was achieved by securing military hegemony. This was legitimately established in the Tokugawa era.

A nation's steady growth depends to a large measure on a smooth power transfer, and the almost 268 years of longevity enjoyed by the Tokugawa Bakuhoo is attributable to the fact that the people's needs of the time were met by the existing system. Maintenance of stability contributed greatly to the nurturing of national power. Even though they had neither advanced science and technology nor modern production systems, the country, paradoxically, used its isolation to create a history of unified self-sufficiency. Most cities apart from daimyōs' hub cities do not have ramparts around them, proving that Japan was safely isolated from foreign invasions. Japan has high agricultural productivity, since most of the archipelago lies in a temperate monsoon area with enough precipitation and ocean currents flowing along the islands, which gives it a year-round mild climate. The introduction of Western technology was an opportunity for Japan to accomplish explosive growth based on its existing strengths including the people's way of thinking, a stable bureaucracy, and a strong educational system that had already been embedded in the culture.

Predestined revolutions

While Japan was accumulating its national energy on the periphery of the Far East, the rest of the world was being swept by a wave of grand revolutions triggered by technological innovation. First, small feudal-lord states gave way to strong nation-states as the development of weapons made war large-scale and more destructive than ever. Nation-states that had already completed integration took the initiative, followed later by other countries, thereby giving birth to an era where the nation-state ruled supreme.

Second, the necessity for public education surfaced in order to boost productivity when unprecedented large-scale war made each country adopt a universal conscription system. Widespread formal education enlightened the general public and the idea of equality triggered social reforms, which promoted civil rights.

Third, new discoveries sparked a revolution in people's ways of thinking. The heliocentric theory of Copernicus, by overturning the traditional Catholic doctrine which held that all the heavenly bodies moved around the earth because God created the universe with humans at the centre, gave rise to the Reformation. The collapse of the authority of the Catholic Church inflicted a fatal blow on the feudal lords, whose basis of power had been religion. As a consequence, all the cultural, educational and social systems were overhauled. The scientific revolution thus shattered outdated conventional thought and further opened the possibility of the construction of a new civilization. It was the Industrial Revolution and a new way of production that empowered Europe to rule the world with its economic superiority.

Japan did not adopt the new thinking that Europe had embraced until 1853, and then it was against its will. Of course there had been contact with Westerners previously. In the sixteenth century, Japan was involved in transactions with Portuguese and Dutch merchants through Nagasaki. By mass-producing copies of the muskets these merchants had brought, Japan was able to achieve unification and secure combat superiority in its invasion of Korea in 1592. In 1638, the early part of the Tokugawa era, there was even contact with Russians who had reached the Pacific coast after trekking across Siberia. Most of these Russians settled around the Heilung river and traded furs. Since furs from colder regions have less volume, and are lighter, more expensive and better in quality, the Russians developed Siberia aggressively. However, the traders were forced to come down to Hokkaido via the Kuril Islands after failing to provide food for themselves.

The Bakuhoo refused Captain Raxman's offer to trade in 1792 when Catherine II 's delegate proposed it to the governor of Matsuma, Hokkaido. The Crimean War of 1853–56 following the Napoleonic Wars of 1799–1815 barred Russia from continuing its eastward expansion. Russia therefore had to be satisfied with establishing borders with China at the Amur river. Europe made full-scale inroads into Asia starting with its trade with China. When China refused to import opium, Britain started the Opium War in 1839, and Britain's victory placed China under subjection to the West.

In the meantime, in 1848, the USA obtained the south-eastern part that amounts to a quarter of its land by winning a war with Mexico over territorial expansion. The USA that belatedly became a 'Pacific power' demanded that the Great Powers of Europe open up, and dispatched a fleet comprising four squadrons centring around cruisers to Japan in order to demand that that country also open its ports. It was an incident that shocked Japan, a country accustomed to previous demands for port opening made with, at most, a few small warships. Japan was completely intimidated by the scale of the fleet.

Admiral Perry warned Japan that if did not voluntarily open its ports within the proposed time, it would have to do so on unfavourable terms, as had China. The Tokugawa Bakuhoo discussed the matter with the daimyō and turned to the emperor to obtain justification for opening the port. Nevertheless, it was not easy for the Bakuhoo to reverse the policy of seclusionism that had been strongly upheld since 1638. While torn on the issue of opening, the Bakuhoo suffered a leak in its sovereign power.

After many twists and turns, Japan signed the Kanagawa Treaty in 1854. Accordingly, the country opened two ports, at Shimoda and Hakodate, and the US consul was stationed at Shimoda. Afterwards, Japan made strenuous efforts to strengthen its national power by introducing new weapons, but to no avail. As the US stepped up its demands for opening in 1858, Japan additionally had to open Kanagawa, Nakasaki, Ikaga and Hyogo. By the time foreigners began to settle in Osaka and Edo (Tokyo) and were given extra-territorial rights, a sense of crisis had begun to burgeon. The whole nation was swept by the thought that Bakuhoo could no longer be an efficient system of rule.

The revival of the emperor

While strong centralism is a necessity for fighting off foreign invasions, this has to be justifiable. There was a need for a national consensus that an emperor should be at the centre of the country's

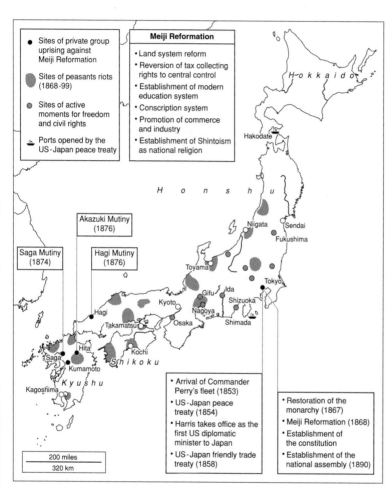

Map 3.2   Japan after the Meiji Restoration

fight against the West. Because of frequent attacks on foreign merchant ships, and terrorist acts against major figures of the Bakuhoo and foreigners, in 1864 an allied squadron bombarded the Japanese coastal artillery corps, forcing open the coastal area of Shimomoseki. As the situation worsened, a national movement was launched to abolish the ineffective Bakuhoo and enthrone an emperor. The Bakuhoo sent forces to quell this, but they were defeated.

It was in the Kansai area, between Osaka and Nagyoa, where the ruling powers of Japan mainly fought over hegemony. In 1615, when fiefs were reallotted, important daimyō of the far western part, including Satsuma and Chōshū, were to a large measure left alone. Two hundred and fifty years later, the descendants of these daimyō rose up to defeat the Bakuhoo forces in the Meiji Restoration. The allied forces of Satsuma and Chōshū owe their victory to the new weapons secretly introduced from the West.

The inauguration of the Meiji Emperor in 1867 coincided with the generational change in the Tokugawa Bakuhoo, thus paving the way for a smooth power transfer. Accordingly, the Shogun became an ordinary daimyō after ceding his rights to the emperor. As a consequence, 250 daimyō came to have equal standing, but only in appearance, since the feudal system itself existed in name only and the real power was in the hands of the samurai who served the daimyō.

The samurai, with the support of the daimyō from the western part of Japan, succeeded in bringing down the Bakuhoo in 1868. Regarding the daimyō themselves as major obstacles to building a strong Japan, the samurai even had the fiefs owned by the daimyō returned to the emperor. As a result, the daimyō came to receive a feudal stipend instead of a fief, and the conscription system replaced the warrior system. All in all, a full-scale policy of national enrichment and security was launched.

The samurai and the birth of modern Japan

Had it not been for the external threat, this series of revolutionary actions could not have occurred inside Japan; foreign demands to open up Japan ultimately united its people. Based on the national consensus that had been reached, a reform group comprising a small number of samurai rebuilt Japan with the tacit consent of the daimyō.

In fact, from 1853, domestic groups in Japan exhibited contradictory attitudes of seclusionism and open-door policies on the subject of international matters. Those from Satzuma and Chōshū thought that it would be better to set up diplomatic ties voluntarily in order not to follow in China's footsteps by learning from the West, at least in military matters.

For several years afterwards, Japan slowly opened its doors and continued to make small concessions to the West. However, in an effort to prevent western powers from exercising extraterritoriality, the Japanese government adopted a legal system and established a judicial institution modelled on those of the West. Also, delegations of military officials were dispatched to various countries in the Americas and Europe for economic, social and cultural observations. The most famous was the Iwakura delegation of 1872. Afterwards, the delegates pointed out that the remarkable economic development of the West was accomplished in a short period of time. Therefore, they emphasized, if Japan were to quickly adopt the strong points of the Western countries, it could easily catch up with them economically.

Here one can see how crucial is ideology. The wheels of history are set in motion when small responsible groups that share an ideology play their part, not necessarily the most intelligent and most powerful individual. Japan is no exception. In 1871, when seven members from Kido, Inoue, Ohokubo, Saigo, Ohokuma and Sanjo co-operated, based on their shared ideology of Confucianism, the group as a whole successfully pushed ahead with accepting foreign culture and reform.

After dividing the nation into 305 prefectures, they recommended that the important daimyō of the west take the lead in returning their fiefs to the emperor and instead receive a corresponding feudal stipend. Afterwards, the emperor called all daimyō to Kyoto in August 1871 and declared a reform measure calling for the abolishment of 273 hans and the installation of 305 prefectures. The incumbent daimyō were appointed as governors in order to minimize resistance. However, at the end of the year, the number of new administrative divisions were reduced to seventy-five, and at the same time most of the governors were replaced by young administrative officials from the four regions of Chōshū, Satsuma, Tosa and Jisen in order to increase control, thereby producing a substantial centralist nation.

What enabled such dramatic reforms without bloodshed was the sense of national crisis shared by the people – that is, there was an urgent need to construct a strong centralist nation so as not to be overrun by the West, as China had been. For the same reasons, the emperors had to be turned into a true ruler. Though the emperor did not have any real power, the daimyō did not have any cause to oppose him. This was the Japanese method of overcoming a crisis.

In 1869 the reform forces issued monetary notes after having set up a strong centralist system. As discussed above, in order to pacify the daimyō and samurai classes, they had been given stipends. However, since the income from the confiscated land did not make up even half of the stipends, the rest of the cost had to be met with newly issued notes. In 1873, tax collectors became the central government rather than the daimyō, and the unit of taxation changed, from villages to individuals. The amount of tax that had been set in proportion to the harvest began to be calculated according to the grade of land. As a consequence, individuals began to gain income in proportion to their effort, thus boosting the willingness for production, so this tax revision dramatically improved Japan's agricultural productivity.[3]

The birth of the economy

A modern national army was established via a conscription order, thus putting an end to intermittent local uprisings. The last uprising, in 1877, started when Ohokubo cancelled the decision, made by the power holders of the Iwakura delegation, to conquer Chosun. Ohokubo argued that Japan should concentrate on its economy and complete national reforms instead of risking attacking Chosun with the Western threat present. Those in opposition to this, including Saigo, instigated an uprising, which was quelled by the national army.

This incident assured the national army, whose inception had triggered the abolishment of social class, of its power. The class breakdown brought about a national awareness that discarded the concept of class. The people, freed from the bonds of class, diverted their passions into accumulating wealth, which developed Japan's economy with great speed.

Japanese merchants, though they remained low in social status, exerted a strong influence. This was because the creation and inheritance of wealth were easy, since Japan was free from external threat. The accumulation of wealth requires free economic activity as a precondition and unlike Korea, Japan was completely free from external pressure or exploitation. What the daimyō exploited (if anything) stayed inside the country, so that national accumulation of wealth continued. In Korea, on the other hand, neither the government nor the people could accumulate wealth. This was because Korea had been devastated since the thirteenth century by Mongol invasions and the Manchu War of 1636. Whenever such invasions happened, a tenth of the population was taken prisoner and a considerable amount of national funds was dedicated as a tribute. Also, because of the seven years of war with Japan, all parts of Korea were plundered, and a great number of its people were killed or taken prisoner.

Commercial capital accumulated during the long, peaceful Tokugawa era, so creating a useful source of funds for waging external wars and setting up a central government. Mitsui, Mitsubishi and Sumitomo, among others, turned into 'business conglomerates', with favours given in return. As mentioned above, the basic structure of modern Japan was established during the Tokugawa era. Nevertheless, it was during the short period of forty years after 1870 that the nation was reconstructed efficiently and systematically by the dictators of the Meiji Restoration.

External invasion by Japan

As a result of a military expedition to Taiwan in 1874, the Qing dynasty recognized Japan's sovereignty over Okinawa, and Japan colonized Taiwan in the Sino-Japanese War of 1894. This war was triggered by Korea's Dong-hak uprising. The Korean peninsula at that time was in a complicated power structure where the Qing dynasty, a traditional continental power, and Japan, a new oceanic force, surrounded it at the same time. The leaders of the uprising that broke out in such critical circumstances were deeply patriotic. Unfortunately, though, they did not have the foresight to note international trends, and the uprising ended as an incomplete revolution destined to fail from the start.

But, the Dong-Hak uprising opened the door for the Qing dynasty to advance into the Korean peninsula and this gave Japan a cause to intervene[4] finally igniting the Sino-Japanese War. Japan, the victor, colonized Taiwan and strengthened its rights over Chosun.[5] While it

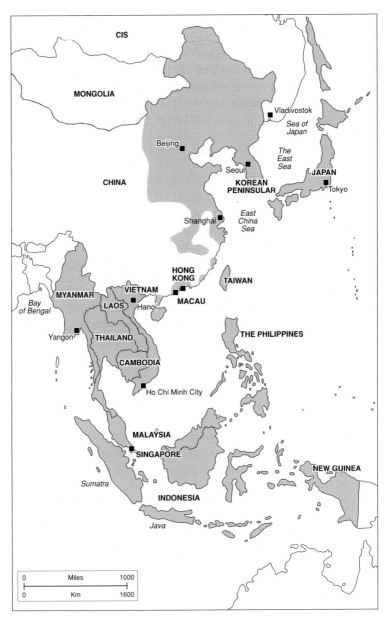

Map 3.3   Japan at its post-Second World War peak

was hampered by the check of the Western Great Powers for a time, Japan instigated the Russian-Japanese War in 1904, based on its increased power. A peace treaty was finally signed in 1906, which was for all practical purposes a declaration of Japan's victory. Scoring a series of victories over the then superpowers of the Qing dynasty and Russia, Japan went further to capture the Liaodong Peninsula and Chosun, securing a bridgehead for continental expansion, but the country, which pushed for territorial expansion by declaring the Great East Asian Region of Co-prosperity under the flag of militarism, was reduced to ruins after its involvement in the Second World War.

The birth of Japanese-style capitalism

British capitalism is based on the principle that an individual's freedom to own and transact is virtuous. In contrast, Japanese capitalism has had nothing to do with such a 'principle' from the very start. As a country with no resources to export, Japan in the Meiji era had no choice but to win over the competition with Western industrial goods to achieve the goal of national enrichment and security. For Japan, a country that had to import competitors' technology and production materials, the only thing to be considered was the need to obey the rules set by competitors. Therefore the most urgent business was to create representative enterprises that could compete with their leading counterparts in the West.

Japan's household industries in those days lagged far behind in capital and technology, providing little basis for modern production organizations, so the state had to assume the task of establishing such enterprises. A state-owned enterprise, once the management was on track, was transferred to the private sector and, as a consequence, encouraged the growth of similar private businesses. Japanese capitalism was formed in this way. As one can see, Japanese-style capitalism is no different from that of the West in that private ownership of production capital and free competition were guaranteed. The process of establishment, however, shows considerable differences.

In short, since state-owned businesses took the lead and private ones were formed after them, even private firms became accustomed to government control. Moreover, before the Second World War, even the criterion for individual freedom or rights was decided by the national goal of a wealthy country and a strong army.

Table 3.1 Comparison of the economic systems of the USA and Japan

	United States system	Japanese system
Basic frame of the economy	Emphasis on total demand Management	Emphasis on the expansion of total supply capacity
Social value system	Individualistic	Communitarian
Corporate goal	Maximization of profits	Maximization of market share and growth rate
Individual view of the economy	Emphasis on consumption Leisure time above labour	Emphasis on saving Finding satisfaction in labour
Corporate priorities	1st Shareholders 2nd Customers 3rd Employees	1st Employees 2nd Customers 3rd Shareholders

Sources: Thurow, Lester C. (1991) 'Japan: The Challenge of Produced Economics', Paper presented at the Havard US–Japan Program, February; Ezra Vogel (1993) *East Asian Industrialization: The Development State, Exams and Exporters* (Cambridge, Mass.: Harvard University Press); George C. Lodge and Ezra E. Vogel (eds) (1987) *Ideology and National Competitiveness* (Harvard Business School Press).

Universal schooling or the health of workers, for example were regarded as prerequisites for securing production for the nation. Even if a business collapsed because of competition, the government upheld its *laissez-faire* policy as long as it did not pose a threat to the national interest. Early Japanese capitalism, where everything was measured by 'national interest' under tight government control, prohibited the waste of resources and contributed a great deal to the miraculous postwar economic growth. There was also a negative side-effect, though. Such a system brought about a justification to pursue private interests through the collusive link between the government and large corporations.

Since the Meiji Restoration, Japan had upheld its policy line of a wealthy country and a strong army in order to overtake the West. Therefore, what was emphasized most was the production capacity of the industries and the long-term promotion of national competitiveness. This process gave rise to production-orientated economics quite distinct from consumption-orientated Western economics.

Post-war high growth

The Korean War marked a dramatic turning point for Japan, which had lost most of its production bases after the Second World War. Japan earned the foreign currency necessary for the economic reconstruction by providing war supplies to Korea.[6] It is a historical irony that a country regained what it had lost in a war of its own making from a war raging in its old colony.

The armistice agreement reached in July 1953 threw the Japanese economy into a deep recession, but beginning in 1955, Japan's economy turned around to begin a period of uninterrupted growth. In December of the same year, the Hatoyama Cabinet declared its long-term goal for growth in the 'Five-Year Plan for Economic Independence'. It marked the beginning of the development of the postwar Japanese economy when high growth ensued. The three periods of high growth are detailed below.

The early period of high growth (1955–62)

The first period of high growth was a time when the nation did its utmost to achieve economic self-sufficiency and full employment, overcoming a shortage of foreign exchange and potential joblessness.

Before the start of the high growth period, the Japanese economy was burdened with two difficult tasks – first, filling the vacuum of foreign income following the end of the Korean War, and, second, providing jobs for the many unemployed, including those who returned from the colonies after the war, and those who finished their military service.

The only cure for the worsened balance of payments was to ban imported industrial goods and to increase exports. This could only be possible by boosting the international competitiveness of its industries, since Japan had few natural resources. Japanese businesses worked diligently towards quality improvement and cost reduction, the cornerstones of international competitiveness. It was during this period that the competitiveness of Japanese products, known for their 'high quality and low price', burgeoned.

If growth rate is kept high to create more employment, then imports of raw materials, half-finished goods, and facilities and equipment increase, leaving the balance of payments in the red. If on the other hand, domestic demand is discouraged, the employment rate will go down in line with the improved balance of payments. The most reasonable way to break through such contradictory situations is to keep domestic demand high while filling ensuing foreign currency shortages with an inflow of foreign capital. The Five-Year Economic Independence Plan was adopted in such a context. Its ambitious goal was to improve export competitiveness to compensate for the decrease in demand caused by the outbreak of a war, and to keep domestic demand high in order to achieve full employment by 1960. The Five-Year Plan allowed the Japanese economy to advance to a higher level through the Jinmu and Iwado booms and, as a consequence, the problem of resource shortages and surplus labour were solved.

It was also a period when the use of durable consumer goods, including televisions, refrigerators and washing machines, spread rapidly. The factors that enabled the people to purchase the goods they desired were lower prices and increased national income made possible by aggressive facility investments by the private sector. This private investment in facilities rapidly promoted quality and productivity, thus reducing the production cost. Japan's formula for growth was to increase production dramatically, based on bold facility investment and based on the income so acquired, to reinvest more borrowed capital in facility expansion.

Under the growth model where investment begets more investment, the speed of production and income increases surpasses that of consumption, which swiftly raises the savings ratio. The surplus income ratio of an urban worker household went up from 8.2 per cent in 1955 to 15.4 per cent in 1961. At the same time, private facility investment ratio to GNP rose from 7.6 per cent to 15.9 per cent during the same period. Over time, such high growth reaches its limit when the supply of consumer durables ends and the increase in consumption demand is at its peak. Nevertheless, with the help of steadily accumulating investments, Japan secured a system capable of mass-producing consumer durables, with quality and function superior to those of the West, at a low price. Taking advantage of the fixed exchange rate system of 360 yen to 1 US$ dollar,[7] Japan increased exports with great speed.

The middle period of high growth (1963–5)

The middle period was a time when the nation laid the foundations for a new way of growth. The most significant feature of this period was Japan's return to the international community. Japanese businesses concentrated on technological improvement and facility modernization under government protection. Foreign exchange earned in this way was managed centrally by the government before being reinvested in technological development and facility expansion. This was made possible because Japan in those days firmly believed that only the winners in future competition would be able to continue strong growth. All possible policies were mobilized, including 'favours' such as financial support and tax benefits plus import restrictions on foreign products, as well as technological developments and facility expansion.

While encouraging fierce competition among domestic businesses in similar industries, the Japanese government set up a system where these businesses as a whole could compete with their foreign counterparts under state control. Japan came to be stigmatized as an 'economic animal' or 'corporate Japan' during this process. Cornered by the ruthless offensive of the supply of Japanese goods, plus formidable competitiveness, foreign businesses strongly demanded that Japan liberalize imports. Though Japan's import liberalization was enacted under coercion, the ratio jumped from 26 per cent in 1959 to 92 per cent in 1963.

The second most significant feature of this period is that most of Japan's large-scale infrastructure was constructed, which also served as a crucial factor in advancing the economy. The Tokyo-Nagoya-Kobe highway was opened in 1965, with the Shinkansen (bullet train) arriving in 1964, which brought a traffic revolution to Japan. The coastal industrial complexes, whose construction began in 1961, gave the country production base superior to those of the West.

The final period of high growth (1966–73)

After navigating the middle period successfully, Japan pushed ahead with its efforts to improve the quality of people's lives and to return to the international community. As the demand for consumer durables that had led the early period of high growth subsided, facilities constructed with borrowed capital became redundant and, 'pressured by interest redemption, the private sector became hesitant to invest in facilities. With the coming of the recession of Showa 40 (economic recession in 1965), Japanese businesses faced a period of ordeals. However, the so-called 3Cs – cars, cooler (air conditioner), and colour TV – created a demand for luxuries thus re-enacting the growth formula of the early period. More importantly, Japanese enterprises established an export-orientated structure, a break from the earlier domestic-demand-orientated model, and the export increase rate was high enough to prevent the country from plunging into a recession. In the case of surplus facilities, the economy was fully capable of utilizing these to cut production costs through mass production, and to export products at a low price. Competitors had no choice but to sit and watch helplessly. With the market expanded and profit margins widened, wage rises ensued, accompanied by increases in purchasing power. This increased purchasing power created additional consumption demand, and this again stimulated more facility investment. These all contributed to producing the formula for growth. Generally, increased private facility investment leads to current-account deficit, but in Japan, quite the contrary occurred, and its current account went into the black,[8] since exports soared and imports declined.

Table 3.2 Major indicators of the Japanese economy

	1985	*1996*
Population (millions)	121.05	125.9
Land size (000s km)	337.8	337.8
Per capita GNP (US$)	11 136	36 531
Consumer price rate of increase (%)	2.0	0.1
Exports (US$ billions)	176	400
Imports (US$ billions)	130	317
Foreign reserves (US$ billions)	26.7	216.6
Economic growth rate (%)	5.0	3.6

Source:　The Economist Intelligence Unit (1997) 'Japan', *The Economist*.

Thanks to the 'Ijanaki Boom' that lasted for about five years from 1965, Japan's economy continued to grow at an annual average rate of 11.8 per cent for the period. Japan's export strategy was to cut costs through aggressive facility investment and to flood competitors' markets with low-priced goods. These strategies have caused serious trade conflicts between Japan and importing countries since then. With the oil crisis in 1973, the Japanese economy, already suffering from cost inflation, an aftermath of rapid growth, and floating inflation because of the excessive influx of dollars, was dealt a heavy blow and its period of uninterrupted growth came to an end.

What led the Japanese economic development for forty years after the end of the Second World War was the dynamism of facility investment by private businesses, but the facilities themselves could not be the goal; they were just a means of production. A tremendous amount of facility investment was made during the high growth period. However, as consumer needs changed swiftly with the oil crisis, the supply–demand balance of the facilities collapsed into chaos. During the search for new targets for growth, facility investment for the 'new era' resumed, paving the way for Japan's domination of the world's hi-tech market of the future.

The birth of Japan, the economic superpower

For eight years after the end of the first oil crisis in 1974, the Japanese economy concentrated its efforts on arresting inflation. The most

62

Table 3.3 Real economic growth rates and Japan's current account after the oil crisis

Year	Japan Economic growth rate	Japan Consumer price growth rate	Japan Account (US$ billions)	USA Economic growth rate	USA Consumer price growth rate	UK Economic growth rate	UK Consumer price growth rate	West Germany Economic growth rate	West Germany Consumer price growth rate	Yen/$ Current exchange rate
1974	0.6	18.7	46.9	0.6	8.7	1.5	14.4	0.1	7.0	292
1978	4.9	5.2	16.5	4.8	8.3	3.6	11.8	3.4	4.4	210
1982	3.2	1.7	6.8	2.2	6.1	1.7	7.6	0.9	4.4	249
1986	2.6	1.8	85.8	2.8	2.5	3.2	3.2	2.3	3.2	169
1990	4.8	2.4	35.8	0.8	4.2	6.4	6.4	5.7	3.1	145

Source: Bank of Japan (1994) *Annual Report on National Economy Calculation*.

urgent matters to address to cure complex inflationary symptoms were to curb total demand through fiscal and financial policies as well as to break the vicious circle of wage and price and to reduce the dependency on oil, while at the same time developing alternative energy sources. Japan succeeded in resolving the crisis and stabilizing prices through close co-operation between the state and private sectors.

The second oil crisis in 1979 did not affect Japan as much, since the country coped with the first wisely. Japan at that time experienced a shortage in domestic demand and, unlike the first time, was under less pressure for wage increases. Energy-saving technology had also progressed considerably. After 1983, when the Western economy resumed growth with plummeting international oil prices, Japan revived its old methods of development, where explosive export increases preceded growth. Instead of pursuing national welfare and international co-operation based on a stable growth policy, Japan concentrated only on increasing exports, thus aggravating trade frictions.

The current account surplus of Japan surpassed US$20 billion in 1983 as a result of skyrocketing exports of its hi-tech products and the surplus growth continued at increasing rates afterwards. The USA called strongly on Japan to regulate exports of individual items voluntarily, to increase domestic demand, and to open up its financial markets. Accordingly, the value of the yen rapidly increased after 1985. Nevertheless, its current account surplus growth showed no signs of slowing. Furthermore, the surplus passed the US$80 billion mark in 1986, and in 1987 Japanese banks topped the international list in net overseas assets.

Trade disputes between Japan and the USA were ignited by the US–Japan textile negotiations of 1971 and the appreciation of the yen. Cornered by the disputes, the USA turned irrationally to the US Trade Act 301[9] in 1986 and the Super 301,[10] a far more aggressive measure, in 1988. Leaving the legitimacy of these measures aside, Japan is also to blame for such a deteriorating situation. Japan, in trade negotiations with the USA, exasperated the latter with its insincere attitude and behaviour, such as delaying negotiations and adopting appeasement measures. Finally, the USA mobilized strong measures instead of friendly recommendations or persuasion and as a consequence Japan became the first to be designated as a Priority Foreign Country (PFC), in 1989.

Table 3.4   US–Japan trade imbalance on major items

Item	Japan's exports to the USA	US exports to Japan	Difference in amount
Processed products	93.4	30.8	62.6
Transportation products	30	3.9	26.1
Vehicles	22.5	0.8	21.7
Vehicle Parts	5.8	–	5.8
General equipment	23.4	6.8	16.6
Office equipment	12.3	3.5	8.8
Metal processing products	0.9	0.1	0.8
Electrical equipment	21.1	6.2	14.9
Communications equipment	2.4	0.5	1.9
Semiconductors	4.6	2.2	2.4
VCRs	1.5	–	1.5
Precision instruments	5	1.1	3.9
Total	95.8	52.2	43.6

Source: The Economist Intelligence Unit (1997) 'Japan', *The Economist*.

What enabled Japan, a relative latecomer, to emerge as a world-class economic superpower in such a short period of time was its aggressive export strategies. Japan declared an all-out war on trade and introduced the concept of strategy to economic development to attack unprepared competitors, as in a war. The country's growth procedures were first to establish export priority industries, pull out all the stops to ensure success, and then to move on to a higher-level industry. However, if Japan, now a country with the world's most advanced technological and capital capacities, still insists on such methods, it will be subjected to strong counter-attack from competitors, who now fully understand the country's strategy.

Japan's role in the New Asia

Japan was the first country in Asia to achieve modernization. Its science and technology and its economy surpass those of the advanced nations of western hemisphere, and it has clearly functioned as a catalyst for the rest of Asia to pursue economic development aggressively. Nevertheless, it must be noted that this was not an international plan on Japan's part, and the benefit to Asia has merely been a coincidental outcome of the country's push for its own prosperity. This can be likened to the fact that Japan joined the Second World War in the name of the Great East Asian Region of Co-prosperity. In fact, Japan is only devoted to an arms build-up without making sincere apologies and compensations to Asia for its war atrocities. Furthermore, Japan is not heeding the concerns of its Asian neighbours who have been the direct or indirect victims of Japanese imperialism in the past and are understandably opposed to its gaining a permanent seat in the UN Security Council. Instead the country is attempting to gain the seat through short-term political negotiations. For Japan to become a permanent member of the Council and a leader of a new Asia, it is imperative that the following issues are addressed first.

Japan must issue sincere apologies to its Asian neighbours for its war atrocities of the past

No country is blaming Japan for its efforts to become a permanent member of UNSC with military power that corresponds to its economic power. The problem is that Japan offers no assurances that it will not turn to hegemony, in addition to making no apologies for past wrongdoings. Furthermore, unlike Germany, Japan is teaching distorted history to the next generation through textbooks, and making preposterous excuses for past atrocities including the Nanking Massacre, and the horrific crimes inflicted on the so-called 'comfort women'. This is the kind of irresponsible attitude that infuriates victims and makes it impossible for other countries to trust Japan. As long as Japan cannot regain the trust of its victims, it has to be prepared for strong resistance from those countries in all matters, including the issue of the UNSC permanent membership as well as the increase in its military strength. Japan must therefore first do its utmost to secure the trust of its Asian neighbours.

Japan must actively transfer technology to developing countries in Asia

By the time Japan was pushing for economic development after the Second World War, it was relatively easy to borrow technology because the West did not view Asia as a threat. However, after the economic surge of Japan, the industrialized nations of the western hemisphere became very alert to Asia, making it difficult for latecomers to import technology. In general, technology is transferable from the originating country to other countries phase by phase according to the country's development stage. However, technology, once having entered Japan, remained there instead of being transferred to other countries. By deterring other countries from emerging as competitors through following the technology introduction procedures that Japan itself took, it blocked the synergy of Asia as a whole while delaying its own industrial restructuring.

It was only recently that Japan moved its production bases to South-east Asia, to cut costs, unwillingly transferring low-level technology. But this was only after domestic production lost its competitiveness because of wage rises and the steep depreciation of the yen. Now is the time for the Japanese government to come forward and transfer technology to latecomers systematically and actively rather than to pass the responsibility to the private sector. If Japan devotes itself to developing new technology based on its capital and technological capacities, and at the same time actively transfers existing technology, a chain effect of technological innovation will take place among the latecomers of Asia, finally expanding Asian markets as a whole as well as sharpening their comprehensive competitive edge. Only after all this is done will Japan be a true leader of Asia.

Japan must expend more effort to open its markets

Considering the size of its economy or its balance of payments surplus, there are too many visible and invisible trade barriers in Japan. If it tries to take advantage of these barriers, it will end up facing more serious trade disputes, not only with the industrialized nations but also with Asian countries. Moreover it will weaken the comprehensive competitiveness of Asia and place Asia in a disadvantageous position accordingly. From a wider point of view, therefore, such an action is self-destructive for Japan.

Japan must make bolder capital investments in Asia

With export competitiveness threatened by the rising yen in 1993, Japan stepped up its investments in Asia for the purpose of boosting competitiveness through cost reduction. Accordingly, Asia is now Japan's second largest investment target after North America. Considering the potential of New Asia, and the fact that economic

Table 3.5   Japanese direct investment in major countries and regions

Country/Region	Share	
North America	47.9	
USA		45.8
Canada		2.1
Latin America	9.2	
Europe	15.4	
Middle East	0.5	
New Asia	25.9	
China		5.3
Indonesia		5.0
Hong Kong		3.1
Thailand		2.9
Taiwan		1.1
South Korea		0.9
Vietnam		0.7
Singapore		2.3
Malaysia		1.2
The Philippines		1.2
India		0.5
Australia		1.6
New Zealand		0.1
Other countries	1.1	

Source: Export-Import Bank of Japan (1997) *Prompt Report on Foreign Investment Study*.

dependency among Asian nations is rising, it would be more effective and more profitable for Asian countries, as well as for Japan, if Japan actively invests in Asia rather than in the industrialized economies that have already fully matured. If this happens, Japan will serve as an engine for Asian economic development.

Japan must actively open its labour market

Japan is the most exclusive nation in terms of its labour market as well as its product market. It is understandably concerned about possible chaos in the labour market since there is a considerable income gap compared to other Asian nations and the Japanese labour market could be flooded with foreign labour if it opened its doors. However, the country can make the most of the regular labor import system according to international agreements. Moreover, by opening the labour market to neighbouring Asian nations, Japan could prepare itself for the free movement of labour within the region after the future integration of the Asian economies, as well as improving the imbalance of labour supply and demand resulting from its ageing population.

Conclusion and prospects

Japan was able to grow into the economic superpower it is in the 1990s because it accumulated energy even in the middle of power struggles among the Western Great Powers in the late nineteenth century, and at the same time pushed aggressively for self-reform. Above all, however, it was made possible by the enthusiasm and foresight of their reform forces, who used the threat from outside as an opportunity to solidify internal unity and accelerate development. The considerable national power that had accumulated during the Tokugawa era, the domestic environment that enabled enterprises to accumulate wealth and actively conduct production activities, and the continued growth of agricultural productivity laid the foundations for Japan's economic development. In addition, a variety of social improvements by the government, including tax reforms, currency reforms, and the establishment of the banking system, provided the basis for more aggressive entrepreneurial activities. The state-led modernization measures such as highway construction, steamship building and the introduction of postal and telegraph systems provided a further impetus for economic development.

Economy is a flow of production and consumption. Only when production leads to consumption, can the economy be maintained and the flow further expanded. The core of the economy is human beings, and humans are producers and consumers at the same time. Therefore, to make a country economically strong, an environment where people can produce more efficiently and consume more is required. Nurturing such an environment is surely a government's role. Only when governments play their role can entrepreneurs aggressively fulfil their roles.

If we were to summarize Japan's economic development, it has been made possible because facing a national crisis, the people united to build a strong centralist nation, rapidly constructed infrastructure, and the government launched a variety of reforms and encouraged production activities by taking the lead in creating enterprises.

Economic development is possible only when the people are fired with enthusiasm for growth under an independent government, and not initiated by external forces. There is no royal road to economic development. If any, it is nurturing the overall environment which enables continued growth of productivity and investment. It is therefore desirable to produce target items selectively for export to almost limitless global markets. To make this happen, the domestic savings ratio must be increased. Also necessary for continued economic growth is a supply of well-educated and hard-working personnel; enthusiastic businessmen who are able to combine production elements to market products effectively; and responsible government employees to push for policies corresponding to swiftly-changing global market trends.

Japan turned its geographic disadvantage of being located on the periphery of the cultural and economic sphere of Asia successfully into a geo-economic advantage to achieve unique economic development, but how the country made it cannot be analyzed with simple numbers. If this were possible, the Middle East or India (which are closer to Europe) or China (historically the most powerful country in Asia) should have developed first. In fact, Japan, the most distant from the West, succeeded in being first. I have tried to place the reason for this in an historical and cultural context because studying a country's history is a substantial task that involves analysis of qualitative features and future possibilities not reflected in statistical figures.

Japan is a country that has, to the time of writing, devised a most successful formula for growth. However, if Japan avoids technology transfer, insisting on maintaining its old practices, its industrial structure will lose vitality and market expansion will slow down, finally causing a collapse in productivity and profitability. Japan successfully overcame the soaring yen and the chaos caused by the bursting of its bubble economy. Nevertheless, systematic checks by industrialized nations, limits to growth facing Asian economies, and fierce competition with hi-tech priority products of competitors will present formidable obstacles to Japan.

Before it is too late, Japan must place its roots more deeply in Asia. Japan, though saying it carries out Asia-orientated policies, overlooks the advantages of the partnership and further trades on the sacrifices of the rest of Asia. As a result, Japan is weakening Asia as a whole. Even if it is equipped with military power comparable to its economic capacity, without the support of neighbouring countries, Japan can only cause an arms race in Asia rather than build up true power to exert influence in the region. Assault weapons with stronger destructive power and cheaper price tags will give formidable strength to even the smallest nation. Accordingly, it would be nearly impossible to force a country to surrender if it is not in an all-out war situation, and furthermore, the international community would not allow it. The most urgent business for Japan now is neither trade surplus nor military superiority but a vision for Asian co-existence and co-prosperity and the determination to pursue it.

Looking at 1997 figures, Japan accounted for 35.4 per cent of the total loans made to Asian countries by foreign financial institutions, with 87.4 billion US$ going to Hong Kong; 58.8 billion to Singapore; 24.3 billion to South Korea; 22 billion to Indonesia, and 37.5 billion to Thailand.

In Thailand's case, the epicentre of the current financial crisis in Asia, an astronomical 53.5 per cent of total foreign bank loans came from Japan. The direct investment by Japanese firms in major Asian countries shows a similar pattern. As of late 1995, Japan's investment in these countries amounted to 87 billion US$ dollars, with 5.7 billion in South Korea, 15 billion in Hong Kong, 18.5 billion in Indonesia, and 8.4 billion in Thailand. As the process of exporting raw materials and reverse-importing finished products became more widespread, Asia became a huge market for Japan, with a 40 per cent share as well as a source of raw materials.

Under these circumstances, Japan cannot be immune to a collapse of the Asian economy, and conversely, an unstable Japanese economy can lead to serious crisis in other countries in the region. Therefore, whether they like it or not, Japan and Asia have become true partners, sharing the same economic fate. Japan is much too important in economic scale and status to be concerned only about its own interests. The global financial crisis ignited by the plummeting Thai baht in July 1997 shows clearly how interconnected world economies have become.

At the time of writing, Japan is experiencing unprecedented difficulties. The concurrent decline of the yen, stock prices, and the economic growth rate has thrust the Japanese economy into a state of confusion. The stock index fell below the 15 000 mark, and the expected growth rate for 1998 stands at 0 per cent. The reasons for the crisis are credit instability and slack domestic demands. Credit instability stems from the weak structure of Japan's financial industry and the 30 trillion yen-worth of bad debts accumulated since the 1980s.

The financial domino effect started with the bankruptcy of Nissan Life Insurance Co. in April 1997 and has devastated Sanyo Securities, Hokkaido Takushoku Bank, Yamaichi Securities, and the Tokuyo City Bank. Even collecting principals on loans made during the bubble economy with real estate as collateral became difficult as the bursting of the bubbles led to plummetting real estate prices and stagnation.

The problem is that decreased consumption and the instability of the financial sector are feeding off each other. A contracted real economy increases international anxiety about Japan's economy, and further leads to business bankruptcies and higher unemployment, perpetuating the vicious cycle of decreased consumption – credit instability – decreased consumption. A more serious problem is that the cycle is not only limited to Japan's economy but is spreading to other countries, having grave repercussions for Asia as a whole.

Japan is also accused of being the 'exporter of the bubble economy'. The low-interest yen capital[11] provided to ASEAN nations since the late 1980s was funnelled into the consumption industries and the real estate sector rather than into production. The bubble economy created during this process and the nose-diving yen combined to give rise to the current chaos. Therefore, at least to correct the situation, Japan must become more active in technology transfer and direct investment. This is not to nurture future competitors, but to lay the groundwork for marketing higher value-added goods as well as to create demand and expedite industrial restructuring, thereby ultimately boosting national competitiveness.

Notes

1. Daimyō: a lord whose owned land is capable of providing 10 000 gokus or more.
2. A goku is a measurement of farmland capable of producing approximately 180 litres of rice.

3. The agricultural productivity of Japan rose by up to 80 per cent between 1878–82 and 1913–17, making agricultural self-sufficiency possible.
4. After the 1884 Kap-shin coup of Korea, Japan realigned its military system to prepare for war with the Qing dynasty, including the formation of a national army of 200 000. The Qing dynasty sent 2000 troops to Asan Bay after the Dong-hak uprising, the Japanese government sent 1000 troops under the pretence of power-balance, clearly revealing its intention to check the Qing dynasty on the Korean peninsula.
5. In April 1895, Japan and the Qing Dynasty signed a peace treaty, approved the independence of Korea and demanded compensation of 200 million ryang, the then currency unit of Korea.
6. The interim foreign currency income of Japan during 1951–3 amounted to US$1.4 billion, which contributed decisively to the economic recovery and the reduction of the balance of payments deficit.
7. Under the fixed exchange-rate system, those who work for trade or capital transactions are free from possible damage from unexpected exchange-rate fluctuation. They can concentrate on international transactions without worry and eventually expand global markets.
8. After having recorded a balance of trade surplus in 1965, Japan's current account was also in the black.
9. When the trading partner violates trade agreements, or its behaviour, policies or practices are unreasonable and discriminatory so that they harm or restrict US industries, the USA may take appropriate action.
10. A regulation by which the USA can negotiate continuously over the correction of trade barriers or market-distorting practices of trade partners. It also allows indiscriminate economic retaliatory measures on the partner.
11. The interest rate for loans that ASEAN banks made to businesses of member nations was about 16 per cent, while it was only 5 per cent for yen funds.

References

The Economist Intelligence Unit (1997) 'Japan', *The Economist*

Kogane, Yoshihiro (1994) *Theories on Economic Development* (Korea: Bupmun Publishing Co.).

Lloyd George, Robert (1990) *Is the World Heading for Asia?* (Nexus).

Lloyd George, Robert (1992) *The East–West Pendulum* (Simon & Schuster).

Song, Byong-rak (1995) *Study on the Korean Economy* 3rd edn (Korea: Bakyong Publishing Co.).

Witney Hall, John (1970) *Japan: From Prehistory to Modern Times* (Dell Publishing).

4
South Korea: The Tragedy of Partition and the Response

A country of wonder

Despite its long history and unique cultural traditions, Korea has long remained in the shade of China and Japan, never coming to the fore in world history, and it was not until the outbreak of a fratricidal war that its existence was known. Korea's history is filled with suffering at the hands of external forces. It's national power was depleted and its army disarmed after having paid tribute to the three Chinese dynasties, Yuan, Ming and Ching; the whole nation was left in ruins and a tenth of the population taken prisoner after six Mongol invasions, while the Japanese and Manchu invasions, in 1592 and 1636 respectively, further ravaged the country. During their invasions of Korea, the Mongols burned more than thirty ships, evicted residents from coastal islands, and banned foreign trade. Korea lost its sovereignty because of technological backwardness, an economic slowdown, and the absence of a global perspective. Korea was divided after falling victim to ideological confrontation. It is a country where 2.6 million people were massacred in the Korean War, and at the time of writing it is the only country where the Cold War still rages on.

Once one of the world's poorest countries, South Korea overcame the ever-present danger of war, and political unrest caused by military coup and dictatorship to record forty years of high growth, aptly dubbed the 'miracle of the Han river', thus, drawing the attention of the world. Continuing on the path of uninterrupted growth, Korea's economy was ranked twelfth in terms of size, the country's

GNP exceeded US$10 000, and it became a member of the OECD, and the country made progress culturally as well as politically. Korea hosted the Olympic Games in 1988, has been designated a co-host with Japan for the 2002 World Cup soccer games, and has set up a civilian government supported by the people.

It is no wonder that foreigners who are familiar with Korea's past consider it to be a country of enigma. Korea has managed to accomplish in just half a century what it took Europeans hundreds of years to do. Since the country's growth has been 'condensed', all the side effects of growth also appear intense and explosive. However, the Korean people coped with these side-effects when they occurred by exhibiting unexpected flexibility and potential. At the present time (late 1990s) South Korea is witnessing the near collapse of its stock market and a drastic devaluation of its currency. The current situation came about when Korea's long-accumulated competitiveness-hampering factors, including high wages, high land prices, high interest rates and high logistics costs collided with the South-east Asian currency crisis that developed in 1997. Nevertheless, I think that once the bubbles are removed and the industries are restructured, the economy will restart the engine of growth.

Development energy accumulated during the oppression

The engine for Korea's economic development has been forming throughout its history. The Korean people moved to the peninsula back in the Old Stone Age, built a nation there before the time of Christ, and founded a united nation in the seventh century, thereby securing homogeneity among its people. In Asia, Korea's history is the second longest following that of China. Despite being connected to a continent, since most of its land is made up of infertile mountainous terrain, the peninsula has maintained its racial purity and a strong sense of identity. With a population of two million a thousand years ago, the country in the 1990s is home to seventy million people, even discounting any specific population inflow. Therefore it could be said that almost all Koreans are each other's relatives.

Throughout its history, as mentioned above, Korea has suffered from incessant foreign invasions, as many as 900 by some accounts. After being invaded by Mongol tribes in the thirteenth century,

Korea was reduced to being a subject of China, culturally as well as politically. Nevertheless, what enabled Korea to preserve its own language and homogeneity was the people's strong spiritual power and sense of identity. However, the ordeals of the people continued. Going through times of extreme hardship caused by external forces, including Japanese colonial rule and the Korean War, Korea accumulated strong internal energy, and a reactionary response burst out in the form of economic development.

In fact, for Korea, development was a matter of survival, not of choice. Small land area, limited resources, long and cold winters, and an increasing population combined to make survival possible only for those who worked diligently. Also, because of a small domestic market, the people had to produce and export all kinds of products to maintain the status quo.

The best resources: human resources

During the process of rapid economic growth, Korea went through a lot of confusion stemming from a change in values and a lack of guiding philosophy. There are some voices within the society that warn against excessive materialism and mammonism. As Japanese colonial rule put an end to the Chosun dynasty that had lasted for some 500 years, the existing order collapsed, depriving Korea of opportunities to establish a foundation for modern industry and national capital. Without experiencing the modernization process that Europe or Japan had gone through, Korea was thrust abruptly into the modern era from its absolute monarchy of over 1000 years.

With the downfall of Chosun and the accompanying collapse of the strict institution of social class, Korea experienced a period of confusing values. Ideological confrontation and war after the liberation from Japan destroyed existing authority. Families with a long tradition and the ruling class of yester-year were no more subjects of respect. Only money mattered in order to survive in a situation where everything was uncertain. The American democracy introduced by US troops penetrated the vacuum of absolute authority, intensifying the trend toward grass-roots capitalism. Those who in the past belonged to the lower class could enhance their social status by accumulating wealth through hard work or education. In economic terms, such a breakdown of class served as a core factor for development.

In short, infinite opportunities were available to individuals. It became widely agreed among people that studying hard was the short cut to making money or gaining worldly success. Combined with a traditional respect for academics, this gave rise to strong educational enthusiasm, which subsequently mass-produced a quality workforce necessary for future economic development. Such enthusiasm still remains strong. The standard of Korean education is very high. Though Korea is not very strong in basic science and technology, it ranks along-side Japan at the top in the world in terms of average educational standard.

Among the remains of its traditional society, one that has had the most impact on modern-day economic growth is the heritage of brilliant inventions and innovations. Korea, in fact, is rich in historically significant inventions. Examples include metal printing (1232), which was 200 years ahead of Gutenberg's; the world's first pluviometer (1442); the world's oldest recording device for rainfall; Palmandaejangkyeong, the world's most advanced woodblock engraving (1251); the turtle-shaped Keobuksun, the world's first iron warship (1592); Hangul, the Korean alphabet extolled by many linguists as the world's most scientific (1443); the world's first suspension bridge, built over the Imjin River in the fifteenth century, and the North-east Asian maritime trading network formed hundreds of years ahead of Europe by Chang Bo-ko, with Chunghaejin as the hub (828–46). This splendid cultural heritage serves as a well spring of quality human resources.

The economic model of Korean-style capitalism

The Korean economy still exhibits strong socialist elements. The reasons for this are summarized below. First, modern production facilities and economics were introduced by Japan, whose economics was in turn mainly influenced by Marxist economics. Though modern economics was introduced by the USA after the Liberation, Korea came under the strong influence of Japanese economics after the normalization of Korean–Japanese diplomatic ties in 1965. Therefore, the fabric of the Korean economy was mainly based on socialist elements. Second, unlike the basic American ideology of individualism, Japan and Korea respect communitarianism stemming from Confucian patriarchism. Third, the long-standing confrontation with North

Table 4.1   Comparison between US and East-Asian capitalism

	USA	East Asia including South Korea
Basic ideology	• Equal opportunities and competition • Material abundance and diligence	Ignoring individualism Duty and co-operation inside community Materials are a means for human relationships
Economic agents Individual Government	Importance of individual competition Small government with minimal intervention in business	Importance of harmony within community State duty of national welfare and guidance
Market	Domestic over international Importance of consumer values (individualistic consumption) Non-humanistic and contractual relations	International over domestic Importance of producer values (communitarianistic production) Transactions as part of continuing human relationship
State-business relationship	Contractual and formal Decision by majority	Non-constructual and informal Decision by few experts representing community

Source: Song, Byong-rak (1995) *Study on Korean Economy*, 3rd edn (Korea: Bakyong Publishing Co.).

Korea as well as the need to justify military dictatorship enabled socialist elements to take root. Above all, however, there was a tacit consensus deep-rooted among people that all should enjoy a similar standard of living, since they had been equally poor and starving under colonial rule and through incessant wars.

In essence, the way of Korean capitalism is to 'allow private ownership' and solve economic problems through the market system. Therefore, it is very different from Communism, where property is shared and basic economic problems are settled through government control. However, it is true that Korea, like the USA and Japan, recognizes ownership by the government or state-owned enterprises. In solving economic problems, though based on the market system, Korea turns in many cases to government control.

To accomplish high growth in a short period of time, Korea also put emphasis on communal productivity, as did Japan. Consumption-orientated Westerners firmly believed that individual consumption should be encouraged even at the cost of corporate investment, whereas Koreans and Japanese hold the opposite view on investment and consumption. Its historic and cultural background put the Korean economy somewhere between the USA and Japan, though a little closer to the latter. The two largest trading partners of Korea are America and Japan. Such US–Japan-orientated structure has long been maintained, leaving Korea influenced by both countries.

Microeconomic factors of successful economic growth

At any rate, the Korean government was able to push strongly for its export-led economic policy under the unique free economic system and national consensus. Distribution of resources was also efficiently conducted by a market system based on the free capitalistic framework.

Some macroeconomic factors that had brought about Korea's economic surge have been discussed. Now I shall consider the microeconomic factors. First, population. Though rather insignificant in number, a population of forty-five million is enough to surpass critical mass for economic growth. This is interpreted as securing a domestic market that enables the development of new export products. In line with this, South Korea should maintain its export-orientated economic structure by continuing to tap neighbouring markets in East Asia, including North Korea, while solidifying its domestic market.

Second, high educational levels, together with the willingness to work hard and a spirit of challenge, which are all very important to economic growth. The willingness to work hard stems from the national consciousness and education. Some say that the Japanese education system is old-fashioned and narrow-minded. However, no one denies that it was this very system that enabled the nation to become the world's second strongest economic power. Maintaining order, not troubling others, co-operating, sharing pain, equality, gratitude to society, and national order and authority as an absolute element for survival – all these are learned in Japanese schools. Therefore, rather than relying on a single superior individual, Japanese people exert strong power in groups. Although Koreans are less co-operative and more selfish they, like the Japanese, learn spiritual elements in school.

Third, a high savings ratio. Such a high savings ratio originates from there being insufficient welfare benefits, and uncertainties about the future. In Korea, the social welfare system has not been well established. Accordingly, the people had to provide individually for their later years. There was no choice but to bear the burden themselves in case of accident or disease, which drove them to save desperately for a rainy day. Despite poorly managed housing finance, Korea's home ownership ratio increased considerably

Table 4.2   Savings ratios as a share of GDP, 1994

Country	Percentage
South Korea	36.2*
Japan	31.4
Hong Kong	33.0
Indonesia	30.4
Taiwan	30.8
Australia	21.1
New Zealand	20.4
USA	16.2

Note: * 1995 statistics.
Source: Bureau of Statistics of Korea (1997) *International Statistics Yearbook*.

because of its high savings ratio. Although less-developed housing or consumer finance significantly reduced the people's consumption level, it resulted in sound household management and made the domestic supply of industrial capital easy.

The depletion of development energy

Like oil that is formed over hundreds of thousands of years, the momentum for economic development of a nation requires a long period to accumulate. Yet, once the economy starts to develop, this energy is depleted within a century or so whether the results are successful or not. Economic development is a cultural product representing the collective will of the people. An individual who has enjoyed wealth for long time is likely to underestimate its value, and accordingly become less pre-occupied with it. As a Korean saying goes, 'Riches are rarely handed down to the third generation'. Similarly for a nation, economic growth comes with a price tag. In bad times, it is easy to reach a national consensus, since people are willing to make personal sacrifices. As income levels rise, however, it becomes more difficult. These are the processes South Korea is going through in the late 1990s.

In the times of confusion and starvation after the Korean War, the whole of Korea was fired up with a collective will to live a better life. As a consequence, any extreme development policy or risky measure was justified and at the same time diligence and frugality became a part of life. As economic development continued and the fruits of growth were enjoyed, determination to pay the price for the maintenance of these was somewhat weakened. Everyone was busy securing his or her own share, which caused a breakdown in organizational harmony. This led to weakened competitiveness and slowed economic growth. Once the determination born of austerity weakens, an economy ceases to grow.

Such events have been experienced in all industrialized countries and are now being experienced in the newly industrializing economies of Asia, including South Korea. That is why high growth cannot continue for ever. The most important factors in economic development are cultural background and business environment. First of all, a national consensus has to be reached. The younger generation, having never experienced poverty, belittles the hard work of the older generation and refuses existing values, making it hard for consensus to be reached.

Up until the time of writing, the public sector in Korea has been too small to interfere with economic development. Recently, however, this sector has been expanding and the strong entrepreneurial spirit that pursues every possibility to create wealth has been waning over recent decades because of labour disputes and strict government regulations. It is naturally so because there are no rewards for taking risks and facing challenges. Phenomena found only in industrialized countries with mature economies are occuring too early in Korea, causing fear that a condensed decline might follow condensed growth. The real economic agents are entrepreneurs, the leaders who create something from nothing by tapping into new markets and developing new products. If we discourage and denounce them, thereby killing their entrepreneurial spirit, the economy is destined to wither. Unfortunately for Korea, the economy, even before reaching its peak, is showing signs of a weakening entrepreneurial drive: without another nationwide austerity drive, high growth will be hard to sustain.

In the past, a high savings ratio turned most income into industrial funds, enabling the economy to build an expansive production structure. Infrastructure investment, in particular, contributed greatly to boosting the overall productivity of society. For example, fostering social overhead capital (SOC), such as power plants, ports and roads, improved comprehensive industrial productivity and strengthened competitiveness, thus leading to economic growth. As the savings ratio tumbles, while consumer spending and the number of holidays increases, some of the pillars that have sustained economic growth are collapsing.[1]

Korea has enjoyed the advantages of being a production base for the world's advanced enterprises: that is, by producing and exporting goods using the Original Equipment Manufacturer (OEM) method, the country has been able to introduce capital and technology while at the same time securing markets. Though it was in the mainly simple processing, Korea was able to introduce all the requisites for production at once, and after acquiring the expertise, it raised capital and produced goods at low prices, finally becoming capable of exploring foreign markets. At the time of writing, Korea is following in the industrialized nations' footsteps by transferring its sunset industries to developing countries. Since most of the developing nations are following the same

Table 4.3   The labour environment of major Asian countries

	Wage per Hour ($/h)		Unemployment (%)	
	1990	*1993*	*1986*	*1995**
Indonesia	0.25	0.43	2.8	3.1
Singapore	2.83	3.56	6.5	2.7
The Philippines	0.67	0.78	6.4	8.4
Thailand	0.92	1.04	3.5	1.5
South Korea	3.22	3.66	3.8	2.0
China	0.37	0.36	2.0	2.8

Note: * 1994 statistics for China; and 1993 for Thailand.
Sources: Bureau of Statistics of Korea (1997) *International Statistics Yearbook*; Asia
Development Bank (1993) *Key Indicators*.

development pattern Korea adopted, Korea has reached a point where competition with those countries with far lower wage levels is not possible. Let us take the decline of the footwear industry as an example. Even though Korea's footwear manufacturing technology was the world's best, as its wages skyrocketed, foreign buyers changed their supply sources to South-east Asia, where wage levels are incomparably lower despite the region's relative technological inferiority.

Corporations such as Nike or Reebok concentrate only on creating a brand image by designing and marketing products and they subcontract manufacturing to countries with low wages. Accordingly, footwear businesses in Korea are also moving their manufacturing operations to South-east Asia, but it is highly likely that these facilities will finally be transferred into the hands of the local people. For the time being, the personal relationship that has been built up with buyers will be able to sustain dealings, but as time goes by, those buyers will be connected directly to the local manufacturers leaving Korean firms without a leg to stand on.

Brand creation based on personal technology is a core element for economic development, and a country without technological capacity is destined to fall behind in the long run. Moreover, in the future economics will be a war of value-added, so to sustain continued growth, Korea should nurture hi-tech and high value-added industries, even if only in limited areas, that are capable of competing with any advanced nations. In line with this, large corporations or chaebols (the conglomerates), should close down their fleet management, where

Table 4.4   Value-added comparison of industrial products

Item	Value added (US$ per pound)
Satellites	20 000
Jet fighters	2 500
Supercomputers	1 700
Aero engines	900
Jumbo jets	350
Camcorders	280
Mainframe computers	160
Semiconductors	100
Submarines	45
Colour TVs	16
NC Machine Tools	11
Luxury Cars	10
General Cars	5
Cargo Ships	1

Source: *The Economist* (1989) 'Technology of Japan', vol. 12, no. 2.

dozens of technologically unrelated enterprises are competing for limited resources at the same time. Rather, they should completely rearrange those businesses and concentrate on one or two competitive sectors in order to survive.

Another stumbling block to economic vitality is a welfare budget which far exceeds the development stage and economic capacity. Up to the present, welfare has not been much of a burden on the public sector in Korea. Its proportion, however, is increasing, thereby burdening the economy. In the welfare states of Europe, up to a half of the gross domestic product (GDP) is earmarked for the government sector, and most of this is for the social welfare budget, including pensions for the elderly and unemployment benefits. In Northern Europe, almost half of pregnant women are single mothers, partly because of the over-generous welfare system. Illegitimate children raised in orphanages are likely to give birth to illegitimate children and abandon them in turn to orphanages, thereby perpetuating a vicious circle and increasingly burdening governments. However, in developing countries, where people are not capable of shouldering such a huge welfare budget, the public sector has not surpassed 15 per cent of GDP.

Table 4.5   Proportion of social welfare expenditure by major nations

South Korea	Japan*	USA	France*	Sweden	UK*
9.9	36.8	29.6	45.0	48.2	29.6

Notes: * 1993, 1992 and 1992 statistics for Japan, France and Britain, respectively.
Source: Bureau of Statistics of Korea (1997) *International Statistics Yearbook*.

As the social welfare system develops, people are burdened with increasing taxes. While such a system is good for the inadequate, it greatly discourages the competent and diligent, which in the end weakens national competitiveness. As a consequence, in some European nations their excessively advanced welfare systems fill them with complacency, and drives competent people to go abroad, thereby stalling growth.

Excessive high tax rates discourage willingness to work. Therefore, high tax rates do not necessarily translate into tax revenue increases. However, tax rates kept at a relatively low level rekindle willingness to work and encourage people to report income conscientiously, thus possibly increasing tax revenue. Singapore or Hong Kong, both of which pursue free trade, are good examples.

The number of government employees continues to increase because of the government's lax management and the public sector expands regardless of efficiency, but so far this situation has not been considered a problem because tax revenues have continued to increase with uninterrupted economic growth. However, the public sector proportion in the GDP of Korea has already exceeded 20 per cent. This will become a huge burden on future economic development and is eroding one of the factors that sustained Korea's continued rapid growth. With the welfare sector excluded, Korea's public sector proportion in GDP is as large as that of Western Europe. This is because even though the public sector share of Western European countries is 50 per cent of GDP, when the welfare sector is excluded the proportion is only 20 per cent.

The engine of Korean-style economic development: entrepreneurship

What enabled Asian nations, including Korea, to sustain their dramatic economic growth was the export-orientated economic policies led by state–private co-operation. If Korea had pursued economic development centring on import substitution industries, as did South America or other developing countries, it might have failed. Domestic markets are in general smaller than international ones. If a country protects and nurtures only import substitution industries in order to control a small domestic market, the burden will have to be carried by the people, thus weakening national competitiveness. Since finite resources were invested in priority industries which were selected because of their competitiveness, export-driven economic growth policies could succeed. Export industries stabilized domestic prices and built a positive feedback system to reinvest earned foreign currency.

Korea is a representative case among nations that have succeeded with the system discussed above. Whenever Korean economic development is considered, the role of the government is overestimated when businessmen should be given equal, if not more, credit. It was businessmen who enabled Korea to make inroads into the Middle East or Vietnam, not government employees. Corporations were the first to tap into markets – Hanjin in Vietnam, and Samwhan, Daerim and so on in the Middle East – and established a bridgehead for future government entry. In the case of Libya, even before the two countries set up diplomatic ties, corporations such as Dong-A

Table 4.6   South Korea's major economic indicators

	1985	1990	1996
Population (million)	40.8	42.9	45.5
Land size (000s km²)	99 143	99 273.7	99 313.5
Per capita GNP (US$)	2 242	5 583	10 548
Gross domestic product (US$ billion)	94.3	253.6	484.6
Consumer prices increased rate (%)	2.4	8.6	5.0
Exports (US$ billion)	26.4	63.1	128.3
Imports (US$ billion)	26.4	65.1	143.5
Foreign reserves (US$ billion)	7.7	14.8	33.2
Foreign debt (US$ billion)	46.8	31.7	104.7
GDP growth rate (%)	6.5	9.5	7.1

Notes: 1. Foreign debts were calculated as at year-end.
          2. Foreign reserve includes gold.
Sources: Bureau of Statistics of Korea (1997) *Major Economic Indicators of Korea*; Korea Import-Export Bank, *Sooeun Survey Monthly* (1987) vol. 2; Bureau of Statistics (1996); 1997 *International Statistics Yearbook*; The Economist Intelligence Unit (1997) Korea.

and Daewoo were contracted for large projects. Such is the importance of businesses in that government-level exchanges are initiated
by corporate exchanges. Therefore, in any country, the main forces
behind economic development are the corporations. Nevertheless,
the government regulates these corporations rather than helps them
to fulfil their role. Government regulations on production, various
services and exports became the main cause of cost increases. The
logistics cost is twice the international standard and, in parcelling
out land for industrial complexes, the government is burdening
people by setting the price three to four times higher compared to
international prices.

As the economy expands and becomes more complicated, creating a need for swift adjustment in the ever-higher interdependency
with world economies, it is no longer acceptable for government
employees to abuse their power and control the economy. As the
economy adopts a precise mechanism, it becomes too delicate,
complex and flexibility-demanding to be manipulated by outsiders
with only a surface knowledge. As the government changes over
time, the Korean government should abandon the role it has played
in the past development stage and take the lead in constructing a
business-led liberal economic system.

Korean businesses, with their short history, are mainly managed
by owners. Social ill-will against this is a factor that further demoral-
izes entrepreneurs. Professional managers are considered desirable,
based on the idea of separating ownership from management. As
could be seen in the recent case of Kia Motors, however, so-called
professional managers irresponsibly determined large-scale investment, thus endangering the firm's existence, and were busy maintaining their managerial authority through collusive link with
unions. In times of crisis, management by a powerful owner might
be better. Many industries that the Korean people as well as the rest
of the world view negatively have achieved success in the 1990s in
large measure because of owner-management.

In income distribution, Korea has a more equal system than many
advanced nations, because of its widespread socialist way of thinking.
Therefore, compared to the USA in particular, there is a relatively
small gap between the starting salary of college graduates and the
income level of CEOs (Chief Executive Officers). The income of
Michael Eisner, CEO of the Walt Disney Group in the USA, was close

to US$190 million in 1996, mainly because of a stock option system. Appointed CEO in 1984 when the company was failing, Eisner was given an option to buy shares at the current price in return for successful management. This option would act as an incentive for a CEO to maximize stockholders' property values; he or she would be given a huge benefit in sharing the interest of stockholders.

In this way, the incomes of CEOs are incomparably higher than the starting salaries of college graduates in the USA, but no one complains about it. On the other hand, income in Korea is equally distributed on a downward basis, rooted in the belief that only equality is virtuous and right. It is true that the equalization of income expands buying power, giving impetus to the economy and reducing social discontent. However, if carried to excessive lengths, it can also destroy the entrepreneurial spirit, which requires a sense of challenge, creativeness and superhuman effort.

Readjusting the economic paradigm

The framework of the Korean economic structure is dynamic. Its industries run the gamut from low value-added industries of simple assembly to high value-added ones that require state-of-the-art technology, and from hardware to software. This structure, if properly managed, would be strong enough to surpass the existing economic superpowers and is often cited as a strong feature of the Korean economy as compared to Taiwan. Nevertheless, it would be difficult to maintain such a structure in the future.

To solve the problem of intermediate goods whose imports increase faster than do exports, the Korean government is making efforts to nurture the materials or components industries.[2] In particular, materials or components where Japanese counterparts monopolize the supply should be produced domestically to ensure technological independence. However, policies for nurturing import substitution industries targeting finite domestic markets run counter to global trends. Materials or components industries should be nurtured, considering the prospects of the assembly industry and as part of industrial restructuring. The Korean economy is trying to reform its industrial structure into a high value-added one and to specialize its industries. Nevertheless, the country faces many difficulties because of the weak competitiveness of each industry caused by the shortage of source technology and the fleet management system of chaebols, based on their capital and their dominance of domestic market.

Having already reached the limit of growth in the conventional way, the Korean economy is in need of a paradigm shift, in order to spark growth once again. Korea's geo-economic location is at the same time advantageous and disadvantageous. Located as it is between China, with its potential to become the world's largest economy, and Japan, now the world's second-largest economic power. Though it is hard to compare the two countries in terms of absolute scale, Korea is desperately competing with Japan in almost every industry, while China and South-east Asian countries are catching up rapidly. Consumptive factors such as small domestic markets and excessive military expenditure will in the future become a much heavier burden.

Without any external variables, it would be difficult for Korea to compete head-on with the USA, Japan, and China. Therefore, Japan should abandon its hegemonism-based economic strategies, concentrate on several priority fields and make them the world's best, thereby securing overwhelming product superiority. While readjusting its industrial structure by aggressively developing advanced technology, Korea needs, without hesitation, to transfer sunset industries to developing countries, while constructing an interdependent system. To accomplish these goals, the government should be recreated as a provider of long-term vision, information and high-quality administrative service. Large corporations, rather than complaining that the government always turns to political logic in solving economic problems, should also reflect on whether they themselves are overlooking economic logic. Before criticizing government intervention, corporations should first stop embracing uncompetitive businesses as affiliates, and shifting the burden of wage increases to consumers and subcontractors by abusing their considerable market force.

Much criticism has been levelled at the past economic development process of Korea by both domestic and foreign sources, but this much is true. Korea, though a latecomer, has managed to build a number of large-scale industries including steel, shipbuilding, chemicals, electronics and automobiles. A large part of the credit for this should be go to the strong will of the government and large corporations. The biggest problem of the chaebols in Korea is the indiscriminate expansion into small-and medium-sized industries based on the economic power they have already accumulated. The Korean chaebols should voluntarily reduce unnecessary affiliates and instead, pursue specialization, competing with the rest of the world.

In the late 1990s, the Korean economy is suffering unprecedented difficulties. A flurry of bankruptcies of large corporations leading to the plummeting national credit standing of Korean businesses has shaken the very foundation of the economy. The aftermath of the global financial crisis triggered by the free fall of the Thailand baht caused the won to plummet in value, draining foreign capital from the Korean stock market and causing share prices to tumble. Behind these unsound firms lies a structural problem of the financial institutions including the banks. Political logic mixed with the presidential campaign added fuel to the problem, making it harder to devise a solution. The government is trying to solve the problem of short-term liquid fund shortages through bail-out loans from the International Monetary Fund (IMF), the International Bank for Reconstruction and Development (IBRD), the Asian Development Bank (ADB) and so on. But such measures will not be effective without solving more fundamental problems. Up to now, the Korean people, as well as businesses, had harboured the false belief that 'conglomerates never collapse'. In addition, preferential bank loans have been made to businesses with large sales and credible collateral such as real estate. Accordingly, businesses have been more occupied with devising measures to gain more loans, including sales increases, real estate speculation and fleet management, rather than enhancing profitability.[3] Therefore, the Korean government, before it is too late, should raise the level of its backward banking industry to that of industrialized nations, as well as make businesses clearly understand that a company is destined to be weeded out once it loses competitiveness. And at the same time, the government should carry out bold restructuring measures so as to boost the competitiveness of the overall economy.

The wisdom of turning a misfortune into a blessing

As the hub of global economies moves to Asia, and to East Asia in particular, Korea has a geo-economically advantageous location.

Sharing borders with China and Russia, and with Japan only an hour's flying distance away, Korea is located at the centre of four powers, including the USA and is in a position to make the most of its location. This geo-political location led to the deprivation of Korea's sovereignty at the end of the Chosun dynasty. But today, when the economy takes precedence over everything else, the location gives Korea an advantage of being a logistics centre. Even though advances in transportation and communications overcome spatial constraints, the advantages of position can never be devalued.

In this context, Korea should expand its infrastructure to include large ports, airports, roads and canals, in order to solve the problem of logistics cost, a bottleneck of development. Furthermore, the country should be recreated as a logistics hub of North-east Asia by utilizing fully its natural geo-economic advantages. If Korea combines its role as a logistics centre with its existing economic structure, it will be able to strengthen its overall competitiveness.

However, a strong vision for the economy is needed to realize all this. Korea has so far been suffering from a lack of strong and visionary leadership, thus casting a shadow on its future. Korea still remains in an environment that places political logic above economic logic. Since the local autonomic system came into effect, regional selfishness and political logic have seriously distorted the economy. For example, rival countries are trying to develop a single priority port in order to pre-empt the role of a hub. Korea is currently building Kwangyang port in addition to developing several small ports in the name of equal regional development. Of course, if there were no competition and only balanced domestic development were to be considered, it seems a logical enough plan. In fact, industries such as ports or airports, to which economies of scale and huge pre-emptive effects are applied, are an area of cut-throat competition where only the best survives. The Korean approach is therefore likely to result in a waste of resources.

The world's major shipping businesses unload their transit cargo in a single hub port in each region for managerial and economic efficiency. As a consequence, the rest of the ports are reduced to being used for local trade. Therefore, from an economic-strategic point of view, the Korean government should abandon its political logic and reconsider its port expansion plan. Rather than wasting energy on Pusan and Kwangyang ports, which are geo-economically disadvantageous, the government should construct an ultra-large port in the metropolitan area, where transportation volume amounts to more than a half of the total. The newly constructed port will serve as a main terminal for major shipping businesses and also compete with Shanghai and Taren. If this takes place, Pusan port will not be reduced to simply a local port.

This must be done to rejuvenate the economy, whose vitality is being drained as it reaches the limit of growth. It would enable Korea to emerge as a logistics power in East Asia. Korea, besides being a logistics centre, would then be able to attract local head-quarters of the world's best corporations and venture companies, consequently creating new businesses and maintaining economic vitality.

To make this happen, facility investment is urgent. More urgent, however, is constructing perfect systems. The government should make an effort to remove various regulations completely, construct a free trade system, and try to attract foreign capital. The major markets of Asia are concentrated in North-east Asia, but Asian head-quarters of the world's leading multinationals are mainly based in Singapore. Even with its geographic advantages, Singapore is 5000 kilometres away from the East Asia region, giving it a disadvantage in terms of distance. Despite this, local headquarters are stationed there because of the government's aggressive enticement strategy and open environment. For instance, Korea or Japan imposes a cor-porate tax of up to 34 per cent and has strict regulations, while in Singapore corporate tax is only 16 per cent and it has many advan-tages as a free port. Therefore, Korea should learn from Singapore, Amsterdam and Antwerp rather than from the USA or Japan.

The birth of reunified Korea and its role

The reunification of the Korea peninsula is a very complicated issue that involves not only the two Koreas but also neighbouring powers, including the USA, China, Japan and Russia. The peninsula will in the foreseeable future be reunified, because both North and South desperately desire it, and Korea must build up its economic power to prepare for the sudden reunification.

The amounts differ vastly according to survey institutions, but a universally acknowledged fact is that Korean reunification will come

Table 4.7   Cost of German reunification

Type of cost	Detail	Cost (bn Marks)
Cost of consumption		
	East German government budget deficit undertaking cost	30
	East German debt with the US undertaking cost	30
	East German state-owned businesses' debt undertaking cost	100
	Trust Bureau's corporate management cost	250
	Capital transfer cost	40
	Ex-Soviet troops withdrawal cost	13
	Reinstatement, compensation, etc. of victims under the East German System	16
	Social welfare cost	500
Subtotal		979
Cost of investment		
	Labour productivity and environmental modernization	100
	Environmental clean-up	200
	Transportation network improvement	127
	Energy facility modernization	100
	Educational environmental gap removal	70
	Postal communications field facility modernization	55
	Housing modernization	50
	Medical facility expansion	30
	Agricultural structure reform assistance	7
Subtotal		1 639
Total		2 618

Source: Sejong Institute (1998) *The Unification of the Korean Peninsula from an Economic Perspective.*

with an astronomical price tag. Some Koreans argue that reunification should be postponed for fear of economic confusion and financial losses. Nevertheless, since the costs incurred by partition is huge beyond imagination, it would be better for the reunification to happen sooner rather than later, as long as it is not accompanied by war. Whatever form the reunification takes, if the South is economically incapable of supporting the North Korean economy, reunification will probably not be sustained.

The most important factors in reducing the cost of reunification are the development of the North Korean economy, and the methods and timing of reunification. The more the North Korean economy is developed through reform and opening, the less the reunification cost will be. The more peacefully and gradually the socio-economic integration is pushed for, the less the cost will be. German reunification was a political victory for West Germany, but it posed a huge economic problem. With East–West integration, the economic system of East Germany went through changes at a rapid speed and the economic losses were enormously large because of the lack of preparation. West Germany spent an estimated amount of up to 180 million marks to convert East Germany into a market economy system during the six years following reunification.

When viewed from a historical perspective, the birth of a unified Korea is inevitable. The time when it happens however, will be when neighbouring countries, including China, regard the reunification of the Korean peninsula as being advantageous to them.

The twenty-first century will be a period of challenge and opportunity, not only for Asia but also for the rest of the world. And especially for Asia, which is in the process of dynamic growth, and for Korea, which is facing reunification in the foreseeable future, an

Table 4.8   Economic potential of reunified Korea

	South Korea	*North Korea*
Population (million)	45	22
GDP (US$ billions)	460	35
Per capita GDP (US$)	10 222	1 600*

Note: * Estimates.
Source: Bureau of Statistics of Korea (1997) *Major Economic Indicators of Korea*.

epochal revolution is expected. If so, what vision of the next century should Korea have? While Korea has never ruled China in the past it has nevertheless triggered rises and falls of Chinese dynasties as well as having been subject to events in China. This relationship will continue in the future, though to a differing degree. Therefore, Korea should be prepared for the time when China reverts to hegemony. Korea should remember the fact that a reunified and robust China has always throughout history looked for external avenues through which to dispense its accumulated energy. Another country Korea should be cautious of is Japan – a country that is steadily reinforcing its military power and is expected to become a permanent member of the UNSC. Preparations should also be made for a possible economic and military confrontation between the three powers of China, Japan and the USA. Changes in power structure will present Korea not only with crises but also opportunities. A powerful Korea may be able to mediate such confrontations among the superpowers by declaring political and economical neutrality. Korea should also make strenuous efforts to become a growth model for less developed countries, and at the same time aggressively transfer its experiences to them, thereby participating in the equalization of world economies. In this context, a guiding vision is the most crucial element for Korea at this time.

Notes

1. Savings ratio continued to decline, from 39.3 per cent to 36.2 per cent in 1995. Consumer spending doubled from 650 000 won to 1 395 000 won in 1990.
2. The trade balance deficit reached US$15.3 billion in 1996, more than three times higher than the previous year.
3. Trade balance deficit reached $15.3 billion in 1996, up to over 3 times higher compared to the previous year.

References

Bureau of Statistics of Korea (1997) *Major Economic Indicators of Korea*

Paul Kennedy (1994) (New York: Random House) *Preparing for the Twenty-first Century*

Korea Import-Export Banks, *Sooeun Survey Monthly* (1987) vol. 2.

Robert Lloyd George (1992) *The East-West Pendulum.*

Song, Byong-rak (1995) *Study on Korean Economy*, 3rd edn (Korea: Bakyong Publishing Co)

5
China

China's place in world history

China, stirring from a deep sleep, re-emerged as a true political and economic power based on its long history, vast lands and huge population. Most historians or political scientists and economists have a fragmentary view of Chinese history – that is, they believe modern China was born when the revolutionary movement[1] initiated by Sun Yat-sen terminated the extreme corruption of the late Qing dynasty, and present-day China was founded by the Communist Party. This is a very narrow view. China is too complicated to be described in such a simple way.

Ever since China boldly abandoned its socialist economic system and adopted a market economy, its annual average growth has been an astonishing 10 per cent. Where did this explosive energy come from? It is not an exaggeration to say that the answer lies in its deep-rooted culture, characterized as being commercial and practical. Though almost half a century has passed since the Communist Revolution, such a cultural tradition has remained deeply embedded in the Chinese people. As mentioned above, the economy is closely related to its history and culture, so for a better understanding of China it is necessary to retrace this history.

The unifications of China and its brilliant history

China stretches 5500 km north to south, and 5000 km east to west, and its total land area is 9.56 million km². This vast land is home to

1.2 billion people. Though there are many different ethnic groups in the country, the Han tribe comprises 94 per cent. The country's magnificent 5000-year old culture, which embraced the Huang He (Yellow River) civilization, one of the world's four great civilizations, is evident from the numerous historical remains. An ancient civilization was already established in 2200 BC. A highly advanced civilization that used writing flourished around 1200 BC. In 221 BC, Shihuangdi, or the First Emperor of Qing, unified the continent for the first time and ruled for about fifteen years. The Chinese continent was split into competing regions after his death but was reunified with the founding of the Han dynasty in 207 BC. It was during the Han dynasty that the ancient Chinese civilization reached its peak. Many ideas and classical works, including Simatian's *Chronicle* were products of the period.

The Chinese people have traditionally taken history as a criterion for values, idealizing the past. Therefore, despite repeated unifications and divisions, Chinese history has been able to solidify its basis. Even though the Han ruled the unified continent between 25 and 220 AD, it was not a centralist rule by a firmly established government but rather a decentralized rule by regional lords. The continent's break-up and the ensuing period of chaos were brought to an end when the Sui dynasty reunified the continent in 581. In 618, however, the dynasty collapsed after being defeated by Koguryo in the Great Victory of Salsu.[2] The Tang dynasty subsequently emerged and by 907 had laid the foundations for China's medieval culture. Although the Song dynasty that succeeded the Tang enjoyed cultural maturity, it was a period of political and military unrest.

The fusion of non-Chinese tribes and territorial expansion

A Mongol tribe conquered Song in 1271 and founded the Yuan dynasty, ruling China until 1368. This was a period of integration with the non-Chinese tribes of the north. Before the Mongol invasion, the Chinese dynasties had been centred around the southern part of the Huang He river. With the establishment of the Yuan, a massive influx of non-Chinese tribes flooded China. Only one million of the 70 million total population were of the ruling Mongol tribe, but nevertheless the tribe ruled the dynasty, based on a strict racial policy. According to the then racial classification, the Mongols were called 'the northern'; Central Asians and Europeans, 'the colour-eyed'; 10 million northern Chinese living along the Huang He river, 'the Han', and the majority of about 60 million living south of the Yangtze River, 'the southern'.

Political hegemony and military power were under the control of around a million Mongols and the one to two million 'colour-eyeds'. The Mongols, without a distinct culture of their own, were very active in absorbing the cultures of others. In addition, they advanced thorough mercantilism, leading China to prosperity. They established the first national monopoly in the sales of salt, alcohol and tea. They developed the Silk Road aggressively, and China witnessed a peak in East – West transactions during this period. It was also the period when Marco Polo visited the continent. His visit provided the opportunity for Europeans to learn about Chinese economy and culture and encouraged East – West transactions. Such transactions subsided after the Yuan dynasty because China, with its advanced culture and economic wealth, did not by that time have any urgent need for foreign trade.

The second rising of the Han tribe

The once-formidable ruling power of the Yuan dramatically weakened because the reign of each king lasted only two to three years, and there were always intense feuds inside the tribes. Also, a number of Mongols were building their own power structures outside the Yuan. To be precise, it was not the Yuan but the Mongol empire that dominated the continent. The Yuan was merely a part of the empire. The area under Mongol control stretched as far as Turkey and Hungary to the west. The Mongols were the most formidable warriors in history, with their unmatched fighting power and uncanny organizing ability. Though few in number, they swept across the Eurasian continent like a raging storm, leaving death and destruction in their wake.

The conquered are naturally hostile to the conquerors. Even so, those invaded by the Mongols bore an unusually intense hatred towards them, because the Mongols were too ruthless in invading and too cruel in dealing with dissidents. Moreover, after conquering a country, the Mongols would place the forces of the defeated before them as human shields when invading another country. The

Mongols themselves stayed behind as supervisors while the invaded were forced to fight until death.

The Yuan attempted to invade Japan twice, with Koryo at the forefront, but, as discussed earlier, these attempts ultimately failed because of typhoons. However, the Mongol invasions forced changes within Japan, resulting in the collapse of the Kamakura Bakuhoo. But the failed invasions also expedited the collapse of the Yuan. Since the Mongols, during the invasions of Japan, placed the Koryo people, one of their invaded nations, at the front as usual, it was Koryo that suffered the most. The relationship between Koryo and Japan deteriorated badly afterwards.

The accumulative effects of such failed efforts significantly weakened the ruling power. In 1355, the Rebellion of the Red Band broke out and in 1368, Zhu Yuanzhang, one of the rebel leaders, expanded his armies and founded the Ming Dynasty which ruled China until 1644. During the Ming dynasty, the Great Wall was expanded and the Grand Canal improved, thus completing the modern civilization of China. Foreign trade was active during this period. The Ming dispatched Jing Hua to the Indian Ocean and Africa with sixty ships and 30 000 crew between 1405 and 1424, and thirty countries became tributary nations as a result. This was a politically motivated action, not trade for real economic interest. If the Ming had pushed full-scale for overseas market exploration, a world civilization might have been formed with China at its centre.

What enabled Europe to lead world history was its pioneering spirit plus sophisticated levels of science and technology. Only a civilization with political capacity and vision can lead history; without these elements, strong national power, a large population and abundant resources are meaningless. Ming's naval expedition proves this: the Jing Hua-led fleet was equipped with all the elements for huge success and was far bigger than that led by Ferdinand Magellan from Europe. Nevertheless, the naval expedition ended being a one-off sabre-rattling exercise without gaining anything of real interest, mainly because of a lack of vision. This is a clear proof of how important the relationship between the will of the rulers and the people; science and technological expertise; and economic expansion are in determining historical outcomes.

The Ming later enjoyed a long period of peace and prosperity, but eventually the dynasty began to decline internally and new forces from the outside triggered its downfall. For seven years after the Japanese invasion of Korea in 1592, Ming dispatched reinforcements to Korea, thus depleting its national power. As a consequence, the Ming failed to quell at an early stage the unification movement that arose in Manchuria. The Manchus were divided into several tribes, and whenever a stronger tribe tried to unify the rest, the Ming would intervene and prevent this. Taking advantage of a timely power vacuum, Nurhachi united various Manchu tribes and founded the Jin dynasty in 1619. The Manchus conquered Chosun in 1637 to eliminate a potential threat. When peasant rebels led by Lizicheng[4] captured Beijing in 1644, the Jin quelled the rebellion at the request of Wusanjui, the great commander, and changed its name to Qing.

The Korean peninsula: a catalyst for change

The Korean peninsula had always been an important variable in the political and military structure of North-east Asia. The Sui fell after losing the battle with Koguryo at Salsu, and the Tang, a following dynasty, was able to maintain its reign for a long time in alliance with Shilla by defeating Packjae and Koguryo. Despite its population being seventeen times larger than that of Korea, China could not ignore the peninsula. Korea served as a buffer zone and the mountainous peninsula was hard to attack. Even if successfully invaded it would have been hard to rule, and the peninsula was economically useless because of its infertile soil. Hence, it was better for China to leave the peninsula alone. Nevertheless, starting with the Yuan, China began to invade Korea aggressively. The Mongols, one of the non-Chinese northern tribes, did not have to worry about forces from the rear, and they had a strong cavalry. It was during the three dynasties of Yuan, Ming and Qing that the Korean peninsula was exploited most humiliatingly and completely.

Territorial settlement and the birth of modern China

The Qing set its border at the edge of the combined territories of Ming and Jin, which marks the present-day Chinese border. The border with Russia was settled according to the Nerchinsk Agreement[5] in 1689. The Qing in its heyday conquered even the western region (in 1759), expanding the territory, but it was weakened considerably because of an internal break-up. Since a small number of non-Chinese ruled the Han tribe, which was tens of times larger in number, the dynasty could not fully utilize people's potential. Moreover, state management was inefficient and social discipline slack. The Opium War in 1842 brought about the final collapse of the Qing. Before its downfall, the Manchu reign was based on the 'Eight-Flag Army'[6] who were given fiefs for hereditary and independent use. The national army was comprised of three eight-flag armies — the Manchus, the Mongols, and the Han — totalling 200 000 troops in twenty-four flag armies. However, as time went by, military discipline was weakened and the economic structure became unstable because the fief assigned to each flag army was sold or used as collateral for loans. Consequently, eight-flag armies were neutralized, which gave rise to rebellions by a religious cult called Bailian during 1796–1804.

Local warlords called Xiangyong successfully quelled cult rebellions, further boosting the status of the Han. In the meantime, Western forces had entered China and begun trading activities. The West had little to sell, but much to buy, including porcelain, silk, spices and tea, thus worsening the West's trade deficit. In the early nineteenth century, China recorded an annual trade surplus of US$45 million. To offset its trade deficit, the UK sold opium to China that had been cultivated in India, and China's attempt to halt the opium trade led to the outbreak of the Opium War in 1840. As a result the UK took over Hong Kong on the signing of the Nanking Treaty, and China suffered a devastating blow to its prestige. The Taiping Rebellion,[7] which broke out in 1850, ravaged China until 1864. It was Xiangyong again that quelled the rebellion, not the regular armies, and this left the country under the control of these local warlords. The central government made attempts to adopt Western technology and create modern enterprises through modernization programmes called the Yangwu programme[8] and the Bianfaziqiang programme,[9] which ended in failure because of corrupt bureaucrats.

In the meantime, on the Korean peninsula, the Dong-Hak uprising broke out. The Qing and Japan sent troops at the same time, culminating in the Sino-Japanese War (1894–5). Defeated by the Japanese, Qing suffered a humiliating loss of dignity, and social unrest ensued. Sun Yat-sen initiated a revolutionary movement dedicated to establishing a republican government in 1911, which in turn gave the Manchu armies, reorganized by Yuan Shih-k'ai, a chance to extend their powers. After the fall of Qing, the continent was divided by local warlords. It was in the midst of such chaos that the Communist Party was established in China in 1921.

In the meantime, Japan, after conquering and colonizing the Korean peninsula, attacked Manchuria. Although Chiang Kai-shek seized control of China in 1928, Manchukuo, the Japan-established puppet state, continued to expand along the coastal areas. To cope with Japan's control over the Chinese coast, Chiang formed the Kuomintang–Communist united front with Mao Zedong. However, the Kuomintang government suffered from internal corruption and weak organizing capacity and was forced to flee to Taiwan when the Communists, under Mao, seized control of China in 1949. China, reunified by the Communist Party, reclaimed Manchuria from Russia in return for its participation in the Korean War in 1950. Reform programmes, such as the Baihua programme in 1957 and the Great Leap Forward in 1958, failed, and with the end of Russian aid, China was left to manage the country on its own.

From equality in poverty to inequality in affluence

As Mao Zedong became weaker and internal power struggles became fierce, Mao's closest associates, including Jiang Qing, turned to the public in order to neutralize its traditional bureaucracy and the party structure. This was the start of the Cultural Revolution. A self-sufficient economy, aggressively promoted during the Cultural Revolution, gradually isolated China from world economies. As can be seen from Table 5.1. China's share of world trade showed a continued downward movement from its peak in 1928 to 1977. To make matters worse, the confusion that followed the Cultural Revolution completely devastated China and threw the country into anarchy. It was only after the death of Mao Zedong in 1976 that China finally restored stability and pushed ahead with its practical economic reform with the re-emergence of Deng Xiaoping, who had once been pushed aside. The year 1978 therefore marked the rebirth of modern China. 'Just like what matters in cats is not whether they are black or white, but how good they are at catching rats, what

Table 5.1　China's commodities trade

Year	Total amount US$ (billion)	Share of world trade (%)
1929	1.4	2.1
1962	2.7	0.9
1970	4.6	0.7
1980	38.1	0.9
1996	290	2.7

Sources:　League of Nations (1930/1) *Statistical Yearbook of the League of Nations*; *General Agreement on Tariffs and Trade, International Trade*, table 2.1; International Monetary Fund, *Directory of Trade Statistics Yearbook*, 1997.

matters to a country is not whether its ideology is communism or capitalism, but how well-off its people are', said Deng, in his 'black–white cat theory'. Based on this theory, he implemented a full-scale reform programme, adopting a market economy with determination and dissolving collective farms.

Such reform efforts changed China in many ways. In agriculture, collective farms were dissolved after 1978 and the farmland was leased for fifteen years, and the term was later extended to thirty years, substantially privatizing the land. Agricultural productivity soared after 1990, when land transaction was allowed. Overall, agricultural production increased more than threefold, from 150 million tons in the 1960s to 460 million tons in 1993.[10] By allowing the farmers to work for themselves, agricultural productivity greatly improved compared to the past, when the farmers were forced into working for the state.

In trade, China's total trade volume in 1996 amounted to US$29 billion, accounting for 2.7 per cent of world trade, surpassing the record it set in the late 1920s. China's strenuous efforts to attract foreign direct investment led to a record high of US$111.4 billion-worth of foreign capital in 1993. The amount of foreign capital, that had been showing a downward movement since then, recorded US$73.21 billion in 1996. In a practical sense, however, it had increased to a record US$42.35 billion, an amount far surpassing that of other developing countries or ex-socialist countries in Eastern Europe. In GNP, the real growth rate[11] recorded an annual average of over 9 per cent from 1987, the year when the reforms began, to

1995. The uninterrupted high growth shrank the number of those living in abject poverty from a quarter of the total population in 1987 to a twelfth in 1994, and increased real income threefold. Boosting such high growth were high savings and investment ratios[12] and the dramatic increases in productivity that followed. Bank deposits of all households as a share of GNP skyrocketed, from just 6 per cent in 1978 to 46 per cent in 1991. Most of these deposits were loaned to the business sector, especially to the state-owned corporations through state-run banks.

The biggest factor that made such high growth possible was China's cultural tradition, characterized as both commercial and practical, but the central government also played its role. It awakened the merchant spirit, which had been dormant for about forty years since the Communist Revolution, by consistently pushing for a policy of reform and openness. Moreover, the government relaxed its control over the entire economy, giving material stimulus to all economic agents and encouraging them to utilize their potential fully.

As mentioned earlier, China's economic success originated from flexible and progressive traits as well as the potential unique to the Chinese people. Compared to the former USSR and the Eastern European nations, China from the start possessed many advantages. First, China was flexible in pursuing rationalization and liberalization.

Table 5.2   China's major economic indicators

	1985	1990	1996**
Population (millions)	1070.2	1155.3	1200.0
Land size (000s km²)	9597	9597	9597
Gross domestic products (US$ billions)	294.3	387.8	697.6
Consumer price rate of increase (%)	6.5*	3.1	8.3
Exports (US$ billions)	27.4	62.1	151.1
Imports (US$ billions)	42.3	53.3	138.8
Foreign reserves (US$ billions)	12.7	29.6	105.0
Foreign debts (US$ billions)	n/a	52.7	116.3
GDP growth rate (%)	16.2	3.8	9.7

Notes: * 1985 statistics.
　　　 ** EIU's estimation.
Sources: The Economist Intelligence Unit 1997, *China*; Bureau of Statistics of Korea. *Major Economic Indicators of Korea.*

With its large population and vast land area, China has had a long history of stable local autonomy and decentralization. Also, since most businesses, excluding the key industries, were led by small and medium enterprises (SMEs), the role of central officials was rather limited. China was therefore able to be flexible in pursuing rationalization and liberalization.

Second, major economic indicators had already been stabilized. At the time of its opening, China had few foreign debts and almost no inflation. In addition, an export market network had already been well-established by overseas Chinese, providing a favourable environment for the Chinese-style 'formula for growth', which is to introduce capital and technology through the network and re-export of processed goods. In this context, Hong Kong was a treasure and lifeline for China.

The return of Hong Kong and its new role

Hong Kong, a port city with a population of 6.3 million, emerged as a world-class city-state ranking seventh in 'world trade volume' and first in 'world container cargo volume'. This was made possible by the synergy between the British ruling strategy, which maximized *laissez-faire* principles, and Hong Kong's economic impact as China's window to the outside world. At the time of writing, however, it is difficult to predict the future of Hong Kong now that it has been returned to Chinese rule (on 1 July 1997), after 156 years of British colonial rule. One thing is certain, however: the giant Chinese economy has gained further impetus.

Hong Kong has a long history of being an active commercial port, but it was during the Korean War in the 1950s that its true value was recognized. With the United Nations' blockade of China, a war-criminal nation, Hong Kong became the only place through which the West and China could exchange information and conduct transactions. China in fact earned a considerable amount of foreign currency by providing Hong Kong with supplies, including food. If that had not been the case, China might have absorbed Hong Kong earlier.

The UN blockade prohibited China from intermediary trade for about a decade. Towards the end of the Vietnam War, Sino-US relations improved slowly, and President Richard Nixon's visit to China in 1972 signalled its return to the global market. The USA was willing to join hands with any nation for the purpose of keeping Russia in check. Therefore, when the end of the Vietnam War terminated uncomfortable relations between the two countries, the USA swiftly reversed its attitude and formed an alliance with China. During this process, Hong Kong once again proved its worth.

During the 1960s, when intermediary trade was banned, the manufacturing industries set up by businessmen who had fled from mainland China laid the foundations for the Hong Kong economy. The opening of China in 1979 rapidly expanded economic exchanges between the mainland and Hong Kong, dramatically increasing the trade volume 54.7-fold over eighteen years.[13] The Hong Kong businesses that had tapped into neighbouring regions such as Guangdong and Fujian utilized cheap labour there and developed light industries. Consequently, Hong Kong achieved high growth as a Chinese intermediary trade centre.

The implications of Hong Kong's success is that even a nation with few natural resources can accomplish high growth as long as an environment for free economic activity is forged. The economic miracle that Hong Kong created from extreme economic backwardness during the fifty years up to the 1990s is a model case of economic development for the underdeveloped world.

In a nutshell, Hong Kong's incredible growth, made possible by maximizing the strength of 'free trade', was triggered by the loss of the mainland in 1949. Those who could not flee to Taiwan with the Kuomintang came to Hong Kong. Businessmen from Shanghai, in particular, set up the textile industry, which provided the basis for the economy.

In China at that time, the basic manufacturing industries were too unstable to export or import. Hong Kong, now an international hub of finance and intermediary trade, had to begin its foreign trade based on simple light industries. At that time, textile products accounted for over-half of total trade volume. As Korea and Taiwan entered the textile industries, Hong Kong diversified the priority industries into toys, wigs, artificial flowers, electronic goods, rubber goods, and so on. In fact, Korea and Taiwan tapped into the international market by selling imitations of Japanese or Hong Kong products at lower prices. Hong Kong noted the trend of the export market, and fostered competitive manufacturing industries accordingly, faster than any other

Table 5.3   Hong Kong's major economic indicators

	1985	1990	1996
Population (millions)	5.5	5.7	6.3
Gross domestic products (US$ billion)	33.5	74.8	154.8
Consumer price rate of increase (%)	3.5	9.8	6.0
Exports (US$ billion)	30.2	82.1	183.5
Imports (US$ billion)	29.7	82.5	198.4
GDP growth rate (%)	–0.1	3.4	4.7

Sources: The Economist Intelligence Unit (1997) *Hong Kong*; Bureau of Statistics of Korea, *Major Economic Indicators of Korea*.

Asian nation except Japan. In Hong Kong, a free trade nation, there are basically no taxes except for some imposed on alcohol and tobacco, which makes it a perfect place for intermediary trade.

In Hong Kong, most of the manufacturing industries are managed on a subcontract system and wages are hourly paid. There are no unions and it was not until recently that the concept of 'minimum working hours' was introduced.[14] In short, the perfect *laissez-faire* system kept the country in order and well-balanced. In addition, because the labour market is completely controlled by supply and demand, the minimum wage level is higher compared to other countries with a legal minimum wage system.

After the Second World War the Hong Kong population surged from 1.5 million to 6.3 million. Even though most were refugees at that time, the per capita GNP in the 1990s is second only to Japan in Asia. The fact that a mere city-state whose land area was too small for farming and whose drinking water was bought from China can reach such high income level proves how strongly market-based free competition among businesses propels development.

The annual average real economic growth rate of Hong Kong during 1961–93 stood at about 7.3 per cent, raising the living standard by more than five times over the three decades. Moreover, since many Hong Kong businesses invested in Guangdong, especially in the Shimchun free trade zone, for re-exports, gross natural product (GNP) has been higher than GDP.[15] The annual average economic growth rate of Hong Kong was just 5.9 per cent but the contribution of productivity improvement to economic development is higher compared to other newly industrializing countries (NICs). In the case of Taiwan,

South Korea and Singapore, economic growth was characterized by productivity improvements stemming from labour increases, while in Hong Kong, already at the economic take-off stage, productivity improvement resulted from income increases. In this sense, Hong Kong had shown the most solid growth among the NICs.

In essence, Hong Kong's economic development is a miracle created by strict *laissez-faire* policies. The government was in a unique situation quite different from other nations. First of all, Hong Kong was a colony. The government, therefore, neither wanted to nor had to create a budget deficit in order to boost employment. The British government always tried to keep the budget in the black, resulting in healthy budget management. In addition, Hong Kong was destined to be returned to China, so everything was managed on a limited basis and the residents were only interested in making money until their planned emigration. All this led to little political desire, and consequently to inactive union activities. Among the total number of workers, union members accounted for just 20 per cent.[16]

Second, most Hong Kong businesses are family-based small enterprises. The proportion of manufacturing companies with fewer than ten employees went up from 62 per cent of the total in 1974 to 76 per cent in 1993. In the case of companies with fewer than twenty employees, the proportion increased from 76 per cent in 1973 to 87 per cent in 1993. Wage levels in South China, where most Hong Kong manufacturers were conducting business, was just a twentieth of that of Hong Kong. Moreover, most of the population were refugees, therefore less likely to initiate labour disputes. They were grateful to be living in Hong Kong and interested only in bringing in the families left behind in mainland China. They were therefore easy to deal with. All these characteristics of Hong Kong provided the basis for smooth economic growth. For Hong Kong, a free-trade nation, everything was determined by external variables, so that its only choice was to adapt effectively to swift changes in its environment.

Since Korean or Taiwanese-style government-led industry nurturing could not be applied to Hong Kong, the only choice open to the Hong Kong government was a *laissez-faire* policy. Ironically, such *laissez-faire* attitude by the government was the decisive factor in Hong Kong's economic miracle. The government maintained a balanced budget; currency volume and foreign exchange were freely controlled; and even a central bank did not exist. Resource distribution as well as wage adjustment were left in private hands. While the government provided only basic public services, such as policing, it regulated land distribution strictly. Hong Kong's colonial administration adhered to a system of land distribution by inviting bids from real estate developers during appointed periods, a system that was expected to continue after the handover. The Hong Kong economy is highly dependent on real estate. Over 30 per cent of state revenue is derived from real estate transactions such as the sales of land, and priority corporations of most business conglomerates are real estate firms. Also, 50 per cent of the aggregate value of listed stock and 30–40 per cent of total bank loans are related to real estate.

Political unrest that had lasted for some time and sluggish world economies resulting from the aftermath of the oil shock kept the economic growth rate at 2.7 per cent. This slowdown turned around only after the announcement of the Sino-British Joint Declaration in 1984, which pledged to maintain 'one country, two systems' for five decades. However, when the USA raised the interest rate and upheld its strong dollar policy in 1985, the Hong Kong dollar, which is pegged to the US dollar, also appreciated. With the subsequent loss of export competitiveness, the Hong Kong economy recorded low growth rate of 0.4 per cent. The rate recovered, but the Tiananmen Square protest in 1989 threw the Chinese economy into recession, which once again lowered the growth rate of Hong Kong, to 2.5 per cent. The Hong Kong economy is therefore swayed by external factors. This is because of its unique economic structure based on intermediary trade as well as the innate limit of being dependent on the giant Chinese economy.

Another factor that limits the Hong Kong economy stems from the fact that it was a colonial state. The only possibility open to the temporary colonial government was to seek practical interests without paying a high price over a short period of time. The flip-flopping monetary policy of Hong Kong is a case in point. Hong Kong adopted the silver standard until 1935. As the price of silver rocketed, the government pegged the currency to the British pound, but as a result of the extremely weakened pound in 1972, the currency was then pegged to the US dollar. When dollar appreciation caused confusion, the government adopted a floating exchange rate system in 1974. In 1983, when the Hong Kong dollar plummeted to 9.6 against the US dollar, the exchange rate was fixed at 7.8 against the US dollar.

Rather than displaying genuine affection for Hong Kong, the British government was more interested in extracting the most profit from it before the handover. The monetary or infrastructure expansion policies reflect this clearly. The new airport project and port expansion project began hastily on an unnecessarily large scale and at an unreasonably high cost. Though the construction projects were considerably moderated because of Chinese opposition, it would be hard for the British government to escape suspicion that it pushed for the large-scale projects to make a quick profit before pulling out of Hong Kong. National bond issuance is another case in point. Since it maintained a healthy financial structure, the government found bond issuance unnecessary in the past. Yet, as the time of the return approached, the government reversed its position and issued national bonds indiscreetly in the names of various projects. However, because of China's opposition, the government was required to obtain Chinese approval before issuing more than US$5 billion.

The dollar devaluation which continued from the 1980s led to double-digit inflation, a rare phenomenon in advanced economies. The reasons behind this were the state fiscal and financial policy in addition to industrial readjustment. First, the government pushed for austerity measures in spite of the very low average unemployment rate of 2.1–4 per cent.[17] Second, as a free-trade nation, Hong Kong could stabilize the trade goods market through imports while it was impossible to procure non-trade goods, including services, from abroad. The aftershock of such a situation affected even common consumer products.

In spite of such inflationary impacts, the Hong Kong economy recorded uninterrupted growth, mainly because of an economic structure closely connected to China. The underground economy occupied a considerable part of the total economy. The prosperity of China resulted in huge monetary inflow to Hong Kong, and since most Hong Kong businesses maintained their headquarters in their country while transferring the manufacturing sector to the mainland, both countries made huge profits in terms of value-added.

The following are variables that have influenced the ups and downs of the Hong Kong economy. First, a decrease in a quality workforce. As the handover of 1997 approached, political unrest produced about 50 000–60 000 emigrants annually. Most of the emigrants were professionals and businesspeople, and consequently, in the labour market for professionals, demand exceeded supply, causing wage rises.

Second, the decreasing proportion of those economically active. The proportion of those who were economically active fell from 66.3 per cent in 1981 to 62.8 per cent in 1993. The range of universal schooling extended to 15-year-olds, thus reducing the number of minor employees. Additional factors, including ageing of the population and early retirement, changed the structure of the labour market, which in turn caused wage increases.

Third, a lower savings ratio and capital outflow. The Hong Kong dollar pegged to the US dollar maintained an interest rate of 1.25–3 per cent. Inflation continuing at 9 per cent, however, made the real interest rate negative. The consequences were a tumbling savings ratio, consumption increases, and a drain on capital. In the case of Hong Kong with its open capital market, bank deposits made in dollars or pounds had the effect of creating the same amount of capital outflow.

The system was an institutional mechanism established by Britain to extract gradually the wealth accumulated in the colony. In fact, the degree of capital outflow was lower than Britain had expected, for the following reasons. First, an uninterrupted capital inflow from abroad to the free trade country filled a possible capital vacuum; and second, underground funds from China helped. This is why inflationary pressure was felt less in Hong Kong than had been expected. It was China that helped the Hong Kong economy to overcome high inflation and low interest rates. In 1996, the amount of trade between Hong Kong and mainland China totalled US$40.7 billion. China accounted for 91 per cent of the Hong Kong intermediary trade, and Hong Kong's profit in this area was HK$120 billion, which amounts to 12 per cent of its GDP. In addition, Hong Kong operated about 230 00 joint-venture businesses and 80 000 processing factories in mainland China from 1993. Up to 3 million people are employed by Hong Kong businesses, saving Hong Kong some HK$200 billion annually in wages. The number of Hong Kong-invested projects in China total some 1500 00. Sixty per cent of foreign loans to the mainland are made through Hong Kong and the official number of Chinese businesses operating in Hong Kong has reached 3200. Twenty-six companies were listed in the Hong Kong Associated Stock Exchange by the end of April 1997, and funds raised through stock issuance had reached US$26.9 billion. As mentioned above, Hong Kong and mainland China have been inseparable in economic terms. Such interdependency is expected to grow stronger since the Hong Kong handover.

Chinese-style capitalism put to the test

The Chinese government has guaranteed the free economic system in Hong Kong for the next five decades to 2047. At the time of writing, 68 per cent of foreign investment in China is made through Hong Kong and a considerable amount of Chinese exports move through Hong Kong. As such, maintaining the current system in Hong Kong corresponds with China's interests, and dramatic changes are not expected for the time being. Nevertheless, China faces many problems at the moment – an unstable power structure, deepening inflation, an income gap among regions and a malfunctioning capital market, among others. These do not pose a huge threat in the initial stage of development, but the more advanced an economy gets, the more serious these problems will become.

Problems most urgent to China are as follows. First, the normalization of the capital market and the correction of inefficient monetary policies. Second, the complete guarantee of private ownership. At the time of writing, foreign investors are hesitant to make bold investments because of an incomplete guarantee. Third, the privatization of inefficient state-owned businesses. In fact, the deficit caused by inefficient state-run businesses is hampering the whole economy; privatization was announced as a national goal in the 15th National People's Congress in 1997. Fourth, the equal distribution of income. In China, significant regional differences exist and there is a wide income gap between the coastal areas, including Guangdong and Hugen, and the inland areas, which has created much social instability. If the income disparity becomes intertwined with the ethnic minority issue, it could throw the country into uncontrollable chaos. Fifth, job creation and the rapid reduction in the unemployment rate.[18] In Chinese rural areas, there is huge surplus labour, and fraudulent unemployment is widespread, sowing the seeds of political unrest.

However strictly the Chinese government carries out a policy of separating politics and economics, the free economic system of Hong Kong will surely have a great impact on the mainland. There is therefore an ever-present possibility of fragmentation that will split China along ethnic and regional lines if it fails to control the eruptive demands for rights. If this were to happen, China would not have the means or the desire to care much about Hong Kong, whose population accounts for only 0.5 per cent of the total. In appearance, China has absorbed Hong Kong. Nevertheless, as Hong Kong capital flows into the mainland via the Shimchun special economic zone, Guangdong, China will gradually become more like Hong Kong.

Will Hong Kong become more like China? Or will the reverse be true? Will Hong Kong become a treasure for China, or will it play the role of a Trojan Horse and ultimately break down the giant political system that has absorbed it? The most powerful engine that has driven the Hong Kong economy up to now is the free trade system, which is effective only when it is able to cope flexibly with dramatic changes in the international economic environment. It remains to be seen whether the Chinese government, which is accustomed to control, can keep the engine running. Just as the future of Hong Kong lies in the hands of China, the future of China will depend on how successfully it deals with Hong Kong.

Britain protected Hong Kong within the scheme of global power-balance because of its national interest. However, this protective shield was removed after the handover, thus overshadowing the future of Hong Kong. Moreover, most of Hong Kong's manufacturers have moved to South China, which has brought structural changes to the Hong Kong industry as a whole. The proportion of manufacturing industries shrank from 23 per cent in 1980 to 13 per cent in 1992, while that of service industries went up from 68 per cent to 79 per cent during the same period. The service-orientated industrial structure is the main culprit for inflation. More serious, however, is the fact that since 45 per cent of the Hong Kong service industries are in foreign trade, banking and design – areas that are highly dependent on manufacturing – they are destined to follow in the footsteps of the manufacturing industries, should they decline. To make matters worse, production costs in South China, the production base of the Hong Kong manufacturers, are rocketing.

In spite of all these negative factors, Hong Kong can gain an advantage over its competitors such as Singapore and Shanghai if it makes the most of its accumulated expertise, a well-established network, a free economic structure, geographical advantages, and its interconnection with mainland China. Though Singapore is pursuing free trade, its listed stock reserves are limited, its stock trading commission is too expensive, and it is geographically distant from the North-east Asian markets. In Shanghai's case, efficiency is lowered by administrative regulations.

Considering the easy convertibility of the Hong Kong dollar and the size of the Chinese economy, the two economies can coexist for a considerable period of time, with Hong Kong and Shanghai taking charge of South China and areas north of Mid-China, respectively. In addition, overseas Chinese are making strenuous efforts to tap into China. Therefore, if there are no conflicts in the foreseeable future China is set to emerge as the most powerful economy of the twenty-first century. By meeting the challenges of these turbulent times wisely and effectively, Hong Kong will be able to strengthen its position within China.

The overseas Chinese network and the grand Chinese economic sphere

China is the motherland of Chinese nationals dispersed throughout the world following the opening of its markets. China serves as a hub of the so-called 'Overseas Chinese Network', and enjoys many economic benefits in return. The estimated total number of overseas Chinese is in the late 1990s around 56 million. Most are South-east Asian residents, and they wield great economic power within the region. Chinese nationals, scattered world-wide but united in a unique brotherhood, are using China's market opening as an opportunity to establish a world-wide network. The economic impact of the overseas Chinese network was demonstrated in the Tiananmen Square protest, and it will steadily grow stronger. Since the Hong Kong handover, the network is expected to exert greater influence on the construction of the Grand Chinese Economic Sphere. As already mentioned in the Introduction, in Chapter 8 I shall discuss the overseas Chinese in depth as an independent economic group.

China is making the most of this overseas Chinese network to induce the influx of capital and expertise, not to mention boosting exports. The network is expected to become the hub of a greater network; that is, the Chinese Economic Sphere. According to a report released by the World Bank entitled *The Prospect of World Economies and the Developing World*, the size of 'the Chinese Economic Sphere' – a combination of China, Hong Kong and Taiwan – as estimated by its purchasing power is expected to amount to US$9.8 trillion by 2002, surpassing the US$9.7 trillion of the USA and US$4.8 trillion of Japan. The gap will further widen in the 'Grand Chinese Economic Sphere', an economic sphere in a broader sense that includes ASEAN member nations whose economies are greatly influenced by overseas Chinese. China itself forecasts that if it sustains an annual growth rate of 8.2 per cent, GDP will reach 8.6 trillion yuan by 2010, and US$6 trillion with a 1.6 billion population by 2050, emerging as an economic power second only to the USA as a single nation.

Arms buildup and the new hegemonism

The purpose of the current arms buildup is to ensure national security and economic strength rather than for territorial expansion or ideological dispersion as in the past. In the 1990s, countries are making large-scale investment in other countries. Military power is a must to protect invested assets and nationals residing in foreign countries. Therefore, every country tries to build up military power corresponding to its national power. Japan is a good example.

However, throughout history, China has always resorted to military hegemony and invaded its neighbours once the warring factions within its boundaries were united. This is the reason neighbouring countries express concern over China's increasing military powers. This attitude has been in evidence again in recent Chinese diplomatic policies. First, 'Multilateral Appeasement Diplomacy' gives priority to economic gains, and practical interests and co-operation with the international community are highly valued in the policy. Second, 'Hegemony Diplomacy' combines the traditional China-centred world view and power logic. Showdowns with two superpowers, the USA and Japan, are presupposed in the policy. What is most important here is that multilateral appeasement is just a means towards hegemony. In late 1987, China confronted Vietnam over the sovereignty of the Spratly Islands[19] and in March 1988, the two countries finally collided head on. ASEAN nations interpret this as China's southward expansion based on hegemony, forewarning of possible future conflicts.

Ethnic groups and the income gap between regions

In spite of the dramatic growth of the Chinese economy, some observers are sceptical about its future. They point to corruption and the wide income gap between inner and coastal areas, and between urban and rural areas. The urban–rural income gap has been a major problem since the establishment of the People's Republic of China. Farmers and non-farmers are registered separately, strictly regulating population movement between urban and rural areas. In 1993, the per capita consumption level of the urban population was 3.2 times that of the rural population. However, these are temporary phenomena that may occur during the process of high growth anywhere and are not unique to China.

Apart from Tibet and a few other areas, the regional break-up of China seems unlikely, for several reasons. First, China has relatively fewer factors for historial, religious and ethnic break-up compared, for example to the former USSR or the former Yugoslavia. Moreover, the people share the China-centred world view. Second, in terms of a population structure, the Han tribe constitutes an absolute majority. Moreover, since the first unification by the Qing in 221 BC, the whole population has for over 2000 years desperately wished for reunification. Third, the provinces of China are so closely interconnected that in a practical sense no single province can stand alone. Nevertheless, if the problem of income gaps among regions and social classes remains unsolved, serious conflicts might ensue. If the central government tries to solve this by force, it is highly likely to aggravate the ethnic issue as well as resulting in an uncontrollable fragmentation of the country. If that happens, the Chinese economy will be thrown into a long recession.

It was the early privatization movement that enabled China to achieve great economic success, unlike other countries that had converted from Communism to a market economy such as the former USSR or Eastern European countries. Private enterprise produced only

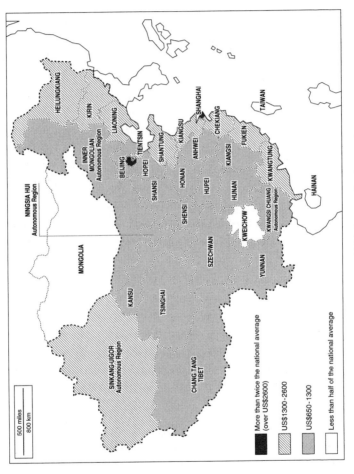

Map 5.1   Income gap between regions, 1992 (per capita income)
Source: Park, Jung-dong (1996) '21st Century of China', *Korea: Economic Daily.*

1 per cent of the total national income in 1986, but with an annual 65 per cent increase, it reached 14 per cent in 1992. The proportion by state-run enterprises fell from 76 per cent to 48 per cent during the same period. With this trend picking up speed, China made the most of its existing tightly-knit, family-orientated style of management to become one of the world's most competitive nations, and it appears that China's competitiveness will continue to grow stronger in the future. If the 'one country, two systems' policy is enforced successfully it may encourage a great synergy. But all will depend on the wise rule of the Chinese government.

The role and vision of China in New Asia

It is true that China is highly dependent on the USA and Japan in terms of foreign trade. Nevertheless, since China has many other important trading partners, the USA and Japan will not be able to sway the Chinese economy at will. In terms of the Chinese export structure, in 1996, 21.8 per cent of its total exports were made through Hong Kong. Of this total, 17.7 per cent went to the USA; 20.4 per cent to Japan; and 5 per cent to Korea. With respect to imports, Japan, Taiwan, the USA and Korea accounted for 21 per cent, 11.7 per cent, 11.7 per cent, and 9 per cent, respectively. China's trade is divided diversely among nations so it seems to be safe from excessive US and Japanese influence. Therefore the USA can no longer control China by threatening to take away its most-favoured nation (MFN) status, as it has done in the past. Also, China has been moving ahead with its capitalist development, dominating the medium- and low-priced product markets world-wide. Jiang Zemin, president of China, who was given absolute power in the 15th National People's Congress, has announced publicly that his country will go ahead and further develop its market economy through various measures, including privatization. If this is the case, Chinese economic development is expected to speed up. In the future, if China joins the WTO, its influence will grow stronger.

Meanwhile, the Chinese ruling elite is making it clear that China will continue to be ruled under a one-party dictatorship. China will surely try to uphold the dictatorship system, just as South Korea and Singapore did, in the name of economic development. However, new needs emerge after some degree of economic development and

China will have to come up with new ideas for national unity and the maintenance of party leadership. It is highly possible that the country will turn to nationalism and consider Japan as a potential enemy. Japan is also building up its military power on the basis of its economic strength to expand its influence in global politics and diplomacy. As a consequence, the possibility of a conflict between the two is ever-increasing.

If the countries of Asia were to become united, it would create a huge political, military, and economic powerhouse that could drastically undermine the influence of the USA in the region. Hence, the USA is intentionally driving Asia into a confrontational structure between China and Japan. In a worst-case scenario, the whole of Asia will be swept into a strife that could shatter its economic foundation, thereby leaving in ruins what has taken half a century to build. To prevent such chaos, China must do its utmost to maintain peace in Asia.

China seems to be pursuing the conglomerate system as well as fostering import substitution industries, following the Korean economic model that gave rise to condensed growth. However, China is in a different situation from Korea, and many are sceptical about whether the old Korean model is still effective today. Every province of China has attracted foreign capital and fostered its manufacturing industries, which has led to a serious oversupply of medium- and low-grade products. If these products flood international markets, huge market turbulence will ensue and, in particular, the manufacturing basis of South-east Asia is highly likely to collapse.

In the midst of China's indiscriminate export offensive and Southeast Asia's desperate counter-attacks, currency values are falling and export prices continue to tumble, thereby worsening trade conditions. If this trend continues, combined with the structural problems of Asia including overcapacity, a result of years of investment, prices will plummet. Also, China has various factors that might stunt its economic growth such as considerable foreign debts, amounting to US$130 billion; unemployment rate increases following the privatization of state-owned businesses; and the reduction of the status of Hong Kong. Furthermore, if the current Asian economic crisis is prolonged, foreign investment in China may be reduced by over 50 per cent and an exchange rate crisis of huge proportions will ensue. China should therefore realize that its economic policy of dominating regional economies through an arbitrary depreciation of the yuan could lead to the destruction of the whole of Asia.

Faced with the economic crisis in Asia, China declared that there would never be a depreciation of the yuan. However, in the black markets of Beijing and Shanghai, the dollar is already being exchanged higher than the official rate and some state-owned enterprises are engaged in the unethical accumulation of dollars. In particular, following the bankruptcy of Peregrine Securities in Hong Kong, the possibility of the depreciation of China's currency is increasing. Should the financial crisis of Asia spread to China, it would have grave repercussions, not only for Korea and Japan but for the entire world economy.

Although the Chinese government vehemently denies this, considering the unique relationship between Hong Kong and China, it is quite possible that the dull stock market in Hong Kong will greatly influence China's economy one way or the other. Also, the unhealthy bonds accumulated so far by the financial sector amount to an astronomical US$200 billion, 20 per cent of China's GNP. If the inefficient financial system is not improved quickly, China's economy will face serious difficulties. Moreover, China's economic growth was based largely on exports and foreign investment. A depreciated yuan will devastate its economy by resulting in a decrease in foreign investment, slow export growth, and massive unemployment.

China's influence will surely increase if there are no unusual changes. In addition, the political map of Asia, and furthermore of the world, will be drawn up by three powers – the USA, China and Japan. In this context, China should be alert to the possible rise of hegemony from within and at the same time carry out reciprocity-based policies as a member of New Asia.

Notes

1. The revolutionary movement: a bourgeois democratic revolution initiated by Sun Yat-sen in 1911, which toppled the Qing dynasty and founded the Republic of China. It began with an uprising in Wuchang in October and an interim government was established in Nanjing with Sun Yat-sen as president. The weak rebel forces negotiated with Yuan Shih-k'ai, a strong warlord of Beiyang with superior military power, and appointed him the new president.
2. The Great Victory of Salsu: a battle where General Euljimunduk won a sweeping victory over the large force led by Emperor Yang of the Sui

dynasty in the twenty-third year of King Youngyang of Koguryo's reign (612).

3. Uprising of the Red Bands: a religious peasants' uprising initiated by members of the Mile and Bailian cults at the end of the Yuan dynasty (1351–66). The rebels wore red bands on their heads as a sign. Zhu Yuanzhang, a major rebel leader, toppled the Yuan and founded the Ming dynasty.

4. Lizicheng: the rebel leader of peasants' uprisings of the late Ming dynasty (1606–45). The messenger-turned-rebel-leader captured Shian and founded the Dashun kingdom. He became the first king and called himself King Xinshun. He overthrew the Ming after besieging Beijing in 1644. He killed himself in Hubei after being defeated by the Manchu troops led by Wusanjui.

5. Nerchinsk Agreement: a treaty for territorial settlement signed between the Ching and Russia in Nerchinsk. The territory was settled at the Outer Shinganring mountains and the Argun river.

6. Eight-Flag Army: a military system set up by the first emperor of the Qing dynasty. Troops were classified into eight groups according to the colour of their flag – Dark Yellow, Stark White, Dark Red, Dark Blue, Light Yellow, White, Light Red and Light Blue.

7. Taiping rebellion: a large-scale peasants' uprising that broke out in the late Qing dynasty (1850–64). It broke out in Guangxi Province, and Hong Xiuquan became king of the Christian dynasty. The rebellion aimed to rid China of its Manchu rule and founding a dynasty of the Han tribe. The Taiping rebels included Christianity as well as the traditional Chinese world view in order to expand their force. Their policy line included equality between men and women, the impartial distribution of land, and the overthrow of the Qing. The Christian dynasty finally collapsed because of internal strife as well as the defeat by the Zeng Guofan-led allied forces. The Taiping rebellion was the first of the modern peasants' movements.

8. Yangwu programme: a modernization programme led by Zeng Guofan, Li Hongzhang and others governors of the Qing, in the late nineteenth century. This was a reform movement whose targets included the military, science and communications, ignited by the Taiping rebellion and the Arrow Incident.

9. Bianfaziqiang programme: a reform movement led by Kang Youwei, Liang Qichao and others at the end of the Qing dynasty. They tried to strengthen state power through the Chinese traditional political and educational systems.

10. Among the major agricultural products of 1995, in million of tons rice was 190; wheat and corn 100 each; and sweet potatoes and potatoes 30, each, respectively.

11. Production growth recorded 3.8 per cent in 1990, 14.2 per cent in 1992, and 10.5 per cent in 1995 respectively.

12. Savings and investment ratios were 40.2 per cent and 41.2 per cent respectively in 1993.

13. China's exports to Hong Kong amounted to US$32.9bn in 1996, 21.2 per cent up on 1990. Exports to Hong Kong, the largest export market of China, surpass those to the USA or Japan. In terms of total amount in monetary value, imports from Hong Kong rank the sixth highest.
14. Average pay per day was US$36 and average working hours per week (manufacturing industries) were 43.8 in 1995.
15. Re-exports from Hong Kong reached US$153.3bn, 85 per cent of total exports, in 1996.
16. There were nine labour disputes in 1995. Participants totaled 1347 and the number of days without work was 1.018.
17. The unemployment rate continued to drop – to 2.8 per cent in 1996 from 4.5 per cent in 1983.
18. The unemployment rate rebounded from 2.3 per cent in 1991 to 2.9 per cent in 1995.
19. A set of islets in the South China Sea. They are mere coral reefs but because of a high possibility of there being oil fields in their vicinity as well as their strategic value, the Philippines, Taiwan, Malaysia and Brunei, in addition to China and Vietnam, are claiming sovereignty over them.

References

Park, Jung-dong (1996) '21st Century of China', *The Korea Economic Daily*.
Robert Lloyd George (1992) *The East-West Pendulum* (Simon & Schuster).
League of Nations (1995) *Statistical Yearbook of the League of Nations*.
General Agreement on Tariffs and Trade, International Trade.
Bureau of Statistics of Korea, (1997) *Major Economic Indicators of Korea*.
The Economist Intelligence Unit (1997) 'China', *The Economist*.
The Economist Intelligence Unit (1997) 'Hong Kong', *The Economist*.
International Monetary Fund (1997) *Directory of Trade Statistics Yearbook*.

6
Taiwan

Taiwan is an island state of about 36 000 km², located just 150 km away from mainland China. In the past, Chinese dynasties paid little attention to the island, which was home to aborigines called the Gosa tribe. Endemic diseases, such as malaria, were prevalent on the island, and because of strong currents and heavy seas in the Taiwan strait, it was difficult to reach.

According to ancient records, the Sui dynasty sent emigrants to settle on the island in the seventh century, and in 1360 the Yuan set up Shunjinsi. However, full-scale development did not occur until Taiwan first became known to the Europeans via Portuguese merchants. The Portuguese who first discovered Taiwan while heading for Japan in the sixteenth century called it 'Ilya Formosa', which meant 'beautiful island'. However, those who actually landed on the island were the Dutch and the Spanish in the seventeenth century. The Dutch landed in the south and the Spanish in the north, using Taiwan as a transit base for their voyages to Japan.

Spain constructed two castle bases, Sandalbador in 1620 and Santodomingo in 1629 in the northern part of the island, but was driven out by the Dutch in 1640. Later, Cheng Ch'eng-kung, a surviving retainer of the Ming dynasty who had fled to Taiwan to escape the Qing, captured the castles and founded an independent dynasty. There were only 45 000 aborigines living there at that time, and Cheng Ch'eng-kung and his followers, including more than 20 000 troops, were the first and largest group of immigrants from the mainland. On several occasions, Ch'eng sent troops to mainland China in an attempt to counter-attack the Qing, but to no avail.

Finally, in 1683, ruling for twenty-three years, he was ousted by Kangxi of the Qing.

After the Qing's conquest, emigration from the mainland began in earnest and the Qing ruled the island until 1895, when Taiwan was handed over to Japan. Most of the immigrants were Chinese from the Fujian and Guangdong provinces who suffered much hardship including endemic diseases and continuous friction with the aborigines. The people of Taiwan in the twentieth century are noted for their diligence and tend to place great importance on basic manufacturing industries such as production. These traits were probably formed during the pioneering days.

The Treaty of Shimonoseki signed in 1895 terminated the Sino-Japanese War and required China to cede Taiwan to Japan. The island then endured Japanese colonial rule that was similar in many ways to the colonial policies of the European major powers. Nevertheless, the Japan attitude toward Taiwan was different in one significant way: Japan cultivated colonies aggressively for eternal rule, which is why Japan expended effort on improving education and developing the island's infrastructure.

As a result, sugar cane cultivation, then the priority industry of Taiwan that had been initiated by the Dutch, recorded an annual production of 1.6 million tons around the end of the Pacific War, a dramatic increase from an average of 30 000–50 000 tons. The percentage attending elementary school reached around 71 per cent at the end of colonial rule; the infant mortality rate was reduced from 33 per cent in 1906 to 19 per cent in 1945; and national income showed annual growth of 3.5–4.5 per cent over the five decades of colonial rule.

From a purely economic point of view, the colonial period was not bad for Taiwan. Though a part of the Qing empire, Taiwan had previously been largely ignored. Serious conflicts between immigrants and aborigines had made country too unstable. Because Japan restored order and built up Taiwan's infrastructure, anti-Japanese sentiment was not as strong as it was in Korea, even after the Second World War. Such acceptance later encouraged aggressive investment by Japanese businesses in Taiwan, subsequently expediting the introduction of technology and export increases of the country. Moreover, the Taiwanese were fluent in Japanese, which further led the Japanese government and private enterprises to prefer Taiwan to South Korea, a country known for its strong anti-Japanese sentiment.

A short history of economic development

Taiwan began its economic development ten years ahead of South Korea. Chiang Kai-shek, who fled China in 1949, swore to reclaim the mainland and based his policies on building an all-powerful state. At that time, Taiwan had some five million residents plus over a million refugees from the mainland – mainly soldiers and bureaucrats. The USA, whose global strategy at the time was to curb the expansion of Communism, actively protected and aided bordering countries.

Taiwan received about US$4.1bn in aid packages[1] up to 1967, including pure economic aid of US$1.5bn. US aid was so massive that it involved 6 per cent of GNP, and a trade balance deficit that amounted to US$100 million annually was solved with the aid of the USA. Taiwan's predicament led the Kuomintang government to reflect on the past misgovernment of the country. Furthermore, it united the country in an aggressive movement to accumulate national power in order to reclaim the mainland. Fortunately, the climate was so mild that even triple cropping in a year was possible; 25 per cent of the land was arable, and the southern plains in particular were very fertile. Sugar cane and rice, Taiwan's major food crops since the Japanese colonial period, became the country's important export products in its initial stages of development.

At the time of writing, Taiwan had a highly industralized economic structure comparable to those of the advanced countries. In terms of the industrial population structure, the agricultural population gradually dropped to a mere 10.4 per cent of the total in 1995 from 56 per cent in 1952. Its first four-year development plan was launched with the help of US aid in 1953 and comprised combination projects that were necessary for both Taiwan and the USA, including power plant construction. On two occasions prior to 1965, the Economic Stabilization Board (ESB) was responsible for devising Taiwan's economic policies. Starting in 1965, full-scale economic plans were developed in earnest as the Committee for International Economic Development (CIED) collected, coordinated, and supervised development plans from all the major departments concerned. Following the successful implementation of this system, the Committee for Economic Planning and Development (CEPD), an expanded form of the Economic Planning Committee (EPC) was established in order to develop comprehensive national and regional development plans and to provide assistance in accordance with the national goal.

Paradise for small and medium-sized enterprises

The Kuomintang government made strenuous efforts not to repeat its past mistakes. Such efforts were most representatively reflected in its policy of fostering small and medium-sized enterprises (SMEs). China under the Kuomintang rule was corrupted by the collusive link between government and businesses, thereby losing the popularity and support of its people. In order not to repeat past errors, therefore, the government upheld an SME-orientated economic policy. Also, Taiwan, with few natural resources, did its utmost to foster an environment for progressive and creative business activities. This is in stark contrast with Korea, whose leaders learned and imitated the chaebol-orientated economic development policies of Japan.

Strongly SME-orientated as it was, the Taiwanese economy was at the beginning not very significant. However, technology and capital accumulated over time finally boosted its international competitiveness. Also, since Taiwan exports highly diversified goods, it does not provoke target countries, which makes it difficult to regulate its goods. Taiwan assembles cheap components efficiently and mass produces quality goods at lower prices. In terms of technological capacity, Taiwan is more advanced than most Asian nations, with the exception of Japan, and a simple corporate structure enables Taiwan to deal swiftly with market demands. Its embedded flexibility also enables Taiwan to purchase cheap components from various sources regardless of their origin.

A solid economic structure

The Chiang Kai-shek administration, through its nineteen economic reform measures announced in 1959, deregulated the trade and foreign exchange sector; unified the exchange rate; and attracted foreign investment, all of which laid the foundations for full-scale development. Subsequently, Taiwan continued to grow at an average rate of 9 per cent annually for some twenty years after the 1960s. In particular, national income rose threefold during 1960 73, with 15 per cent from employment increases, 35 per cent from capital investment, and the remaining 50 per cent from technological improvement. The improvement in technology was largely a result of foreign investment, and later improvement became the model for the East Asian economic development strategy of the late 1990s.

In the 1970s, savings and investment ratios of Taiwan were 32 per cent and 30.5 per cent respectively, and most of the investment was met by domestic savings. In the 1980s the situation was similar. In 1994, however, the savings and investment ratios decreased to 26.3 per cent and 23.7 per cent, respectively. As a result, the rates of economic growth and inflation were reduced from 9.3 percent and 11.1 per cent in the 1970s, to 6 per cent and 3.7 per cent, respectively in 1995.

Regarding the economic structure, the agricultural sector accounted for 11.3 per cent in 1975, but its percentage had shrunk to 3.5 per cent by 1993. Taiwan's cultivation ratio is up to 2.5 times that of Korea because of triple cropping and arable land that occupies over a quarter of the total land area. Nevertheless, its agriculture ratio is a much lower percentage. This proves how solid are the foundations of Taiwan's manufacturing industries. The proportion of total trade in GDP is about 76 per cent and up to 48 per cent is accounted for by exports. This shows clearly how externally-orientated is Taiwan's

Table 6.1   Taiwan's major economic indicators

	1985	1990	1996
Population (millions)	19.3	20.3	21.4
Land size (000's km^2)	36.0	36.0	36.0
Per capita GNP (US$)	3 297.0	111.0	12 772.0
Gross domestic products (US$ billions)	62.1	160.2	273.3
Consumer price rate of increase (%)	–0.2	4.1	3.1
Exports (US$ billions)	30.6	67.0	115.1
Imports (US$ billions)	20.1	54.7	96.8
Foreign Reserves (US$ billions)	22.6	72.4	88.3
GDP growth rate (%)	5.0	5.4	5.7

Sources: Bureau of Statistices of Korea (1997) *Major Economic Indicators of Korea*; The Economist Intelligence Unit (1997) *Taiwan*.

economic structure. Regarding the total amount of exports, the manufacturing sector accounted for 21 per cent in the 1950s most of which was from light industries, but that proportion increased to 90 per cent by 1990, mainly from heavy chemicals and precision industries.

Taiwan's biggest trading partner is the USA but Taiwan's exports to the USA shrank from 34 per cent in the 1980s to 27.6 per cent in 1993, while those to China and Hong Kong went up from 7.9 per cent to 21.7 per cent. Exports to ASEAN nations rose too, from 7.9 per cent to 9.4 per cent. This trend proves that, in terms of trade, Taiwan has moved away from a strong focus on US and Japan to concentrate more on China and ASEAN. It also shows the country's move to diversify its export markets.

On taking office, the Kuomintang government established three goals for its economic policy. The first was price stabilization. Taiwan had suffered high inflation stemming from an astronomical amount of military expenditure as well as from a shortage of funds. Inflation is a big burden on politics and society and paralyzes the market system. The more precise a machine, the more efficient it is. Only when a society has stabilized prices and wages can it function with precision, thereby raising its efficiency. Severe price fluctuations make forecasting impossible and distort the distribution of resources, in the end hampering efficiency.

The second was farmland reform. Tenant-farming gave way to owner-farming and improved agricultural productivity. Collected taxes were utilized for industrialization. However, with the country gaining stability, the government abandoned its import-substitution-orientated industrialization policy. Because fostering import-substitution industries for limited domestic markets resulted in higher production costs and inefficiency, the government shifted to an export-led industrialization policy and this policy was adopted not only by Taiwan but also by the entire East Asia region. This is in stark contrast to countries in Latin America, Australia and New Zealand that concentrated mainly on import-substitution industries. Australia, for example, encouraged the inefficient domestic manufacturing industries with foreign currency earned by exporting its abundant mineral resources and agricultural products. However, such efforts eventually strained the national economy because the domestic market was too small for the industries to be competitive.

Industrial restructuring and infrastructure investment

During the 1960s, interest rates were liberalized, which encouraged savings. As a consequence, any SME could get loans for business activities whenever there was an investment opportunity. At the same time, preferential financing was stopped, boosting investment efficiency and further strengthening competitiveness. During the 1970s, wages were raised so much that low value-added light industries lost competitiveness and this paved the way for industrial restructuring. In 1991, the Taiwan government announced a policy of infrastructure investment that pledged to invest up to US$800bn in 775 projects over the following five years. Though this was later moderated to US$229 billion and 632 projects in 1993, it was still a massive investment.

In 1991, Taiwan made bold investments in high speed trains, information and telecommunications networks and nuclear power plant construction, among others, while adopting policies to develop ten strategic industries: namely, aerospace, communications, information, semiconductors, precision machines, automatic machines, new materials, precision chemicals and pharmaceuticals, medical systems, pollution control and electronics. In 1994, the government reduced the number of investment to five. The government is providing strategic industries with a variety of privileges – concentrated investment; the acceleration of depreciation; tax cuts on R & D costs; pollution control; investments in automation; and the reduction in corporate tax to between 5 per cent and 20 per cent. In comparison, corporate tax in Korea is 34 per cent, which is too high compared to 16 per cent in Hong Kong and Singapore.

Challenge and conquest

Taiwan has made huge investments in order to establish itself as the hub of finance, information, and trade in North-east Asia, but by the late 1990s its efforts have largely failed. This can be attributed to the fact that Taiwan is at a political disadvantage in the global arena. After the division of the country, China had continued to insist on the 'one China' principle and isolated Taiwan politically and diplomatically Diminished political influence in the global arena results in fewer choices and significantly weaker economic stance.

Jiang Zemin of China proclaimed 'one country, two systems'. The policy line for the Hong Kong handover, was a preparatory measure for ultimate reunification with Taiwan, thus making clear China's intention to absorb the nation. Moreover, because the Chinese economy is ever expanding, it appears unlikely that Taiwan will be able to reclaim the mainland. In Taiwan, the people are openly calling themselves 'Taiwanese' and are increasingly calling for independence, breaking the past taboo. The Taiwanese government therefore needs to review the independence issue in depth.

The country will surely face strong opposition and a threat of war from China. In any case, Taiwan can no longer go against the current. Internally, Taiwan should come up with a national consensus, and externally concentrate its diplomatic capacity on persuading the international community of the legitimacy of its independence. It remains to be seen how wisely the Taiwanese government and businesses cope with new challenges after losing a political and economic buffer zone in the Hong Kong handover.

Note

1. According to some statistics, US aid amounted to US$1.5bn during 1951–65. However, this appears to be a statistical mistake made by misunderstanding the kind of aid involved. In other words, US$1.5bn may have been pure economic aid, and US$4.1bn an amount that includes military aid.

References

Chia, Siow-Yue and Cheng, Bifan (1987) *ASEAN-China Economic Relations* Singapore: ISEAS

Mitsubishi Research Institute (1996) *Total Forecasting of Asia.*

Ng Yuzin Chiautong (1993) *Taiwan Chingchi Fachan Te Mimi* Korea: Kyomun Publishing Co.

Pluvier Jan (1974) *Southeast Asia From Colonialism to Independence,* Kuala Lumpur: Oxford Univesity Press.

7
Singapore

Having the world's largest container port and airport, Singapore is referred to as the logistics hub of South-east Asia. Its well-maintained roads, efficient administrative and economic systems, and national income surpassing that of Europe are some of the reasons why it is known as an 'Asian Tiger'. However, it is worth noting that the symbol for Singapore is a lion, reflecting the fact that it is a country of overseas Chinese. Overseas Chinese account for 77 per cent of Singapore's population, and control more than 81 per cent of its capital.

Singapore flourished through foreign trade in the fourteenth century as an important shipping channel linking the East and the West. In 1819, however, when Stamford Raffles arrived in Singapore, it was a mere wasteland dominated by pirates and with only some 150 residents. How, then, could the country rise from such a state to accomplish an incredible economic development in such a short time? Singapore is similar to Hong Kong in that both are successful city-states, but in terms of their development process and historical backgrounds, the two are totally different. Therefore, Singapore is another model worth using as a benchmark for the developing world.

A short history of the birth of Singapore and its economic development

Singapore is located on an island off the southern tip of the Malay peninsula, and has strategic value as a natural port and transit centre linking Europe and the Far East. Struggles between Thailand and Indonesia to occupy Singapore left the country in ruins. However, in 1819, Singapore became a trading centre along with Penang and Malacca. Within three years of development, this former wasteland had grown into a major trading city with a population of over 100 00. This was possible mainly due to Raffles' open-door policy, which enabled Chinese and Indians unlimited access. As a result, 360 000 Chinese immigrated to Singapore by 1927.

Singapore, once managed by the British East India Company, came under the direct control of the UK in 1867. With the opening of the Suez Canal in 1869. Singapore had become a country of great strategic importance. Mutual protection agreements signed with Malaysian sultans enabled Singapore to set up more stable and open economic systems, and Singapore introduced British systems of education, law, and administration, which paved the way for the most productive and efficient infrastructure in South-east Asia. The small size of the country was a weak point, but at the same time an advantage, as it improved efficiency in state administration.

In 1942, Japan occupied Singapore and carried out a systematic massacre of the Chinese. After the Second World War, Singapore came briefly under military rule but was finally able to establish an independent government in 1959, and the long colonial rule that had lasted for 135 years finally ended. As neighbouring countries gained independence and developed large ports of their own, the role of Singapore as a transit port was reduced. In response, the country shifted its economic policy to a manufacturing-orientated one.

In 1961, Singapore joined the 'Malaysian Federation' at the suggestion of Malaysian Prime Minister Abdul Rahman. However, Achmad Sukarno, then regional leader, disagreed with the construction of a strong federation without his participation and sent troops to Brunei and Malaysia, and Malaysia withdrew. Malaysia also did not welcome the merger with Singapore because it would make the number of Chinese equal to the Malaysians. As a result, Singapore broke away and became independent once again in 1965.

Singapore's economy was highly dependent on Britain. In 1968, when British troops withdrew from Singapore for three years, the British pound plummeted, slowing down Singapore's economy and raising the unemployment rate to 16 per cent. The merger with

Table 7.1   Singapore's major economic indicators

	1985	1990
Population (millions)	19.3	20.3
Land size (000's km²)	36.0	36.0
Per capita GNP (US$)	3 297.0	111.0
Gross domestic poducts (US$ billions)	62.1	160.2
Consumer price rate of increase (%)	–0.2	4.1
Exports (US$ billions)	30.6	67.0
Imports (US$ billions)	20.1	54.7
Foreign reserve (US$ billions)	22.6	72.4
GDP growth rate (%)	5.0	5.4

Sources: Bureau of Statistics of Korea (1997); *Major Economic Indicators of Korea*, The
Economist Intelligence Unit (1997) *Singapore*.

Malaysia had given Singapore a domestic market big enough to push for import-substitution industries, but independence changed the situation. Accordingly, Prime Minister Lee Kuan Yew reversed the country's economic policy into one that was led by exports. In addition, he attracted foreign businesses with strong incentives, including a variety of tax exemptions. He also cut taxes on export promotion costs and deregulated all types of fund transfer. Though labour disputes, including strikes, were legally banned, wages were determined according to a law of supply and demand, which caused no discontent among workers. As a consequence, Singapore came to have the most stable labour relations in the world as well as a hard-working and well-educated workforce. Average working hours per week totalled 49.3 in 1995, exceeding the 37.8 hours in Japan and 46.4 in Taiwan. With the higher education attendance rate topping 35.2 per cent and the savings rate and investment rate at 47.3 per cent and 40.7 per cent, respectively, Singapore has all the factors necessary for sound economic development.

Because of these advantages, foreign businesses prefer to set up production bases or headquarters in Singapore even when investing in markets all over Asia. The externally-orientated economic structure of Singapore served as an engine for high growth, raising per capita GNP from just US$500 in the 1950s to an incredible US$30 935 in 1996.

Table 7.2 Proportion of foreign businesses in Singapore's manufacturing industries

	Number of businesses	Number of employees (000s persons)	Amount of Production (US$millions)	Amount of direct export (US$millions)
100% local capital	2 508	102.1	5 942	2 022
Over 50% local capital	329	42.3	3 557	1 669
Over 50% foreign capital	245	35.4	5 436	3 242
100% foreign capital	621	171.8	24 422	18 997
Total	3 703	351.7	39 357	25 930

Source: Japan External Trade Organization (1993) Trade White Paper.

Among the major trading goods of Singapore, machinery and equipment make up 82.5 per cent of total exports and 76 per cent of total imports, leading the economy. The major exporting countries of Singapore: the USA, Japan and Malaysia, take more than a half of total exports while the EU takes 13 per cent.

Lee Kuan Yew, the pioneer of development

The process of overcoming national crisis produced a national hero named Lee Kuan Yew. A graduate of Cambridge University in the UK, Lee began his political career after forming the People's Action Party (PAP). After Singapore's attempt to join the Malaysian Federation ended in failure, Lee established various economic policies to promote self-sufficiency. Singapore has natural geographical advantages as a port and has always been highly valued for its strategic importance. Lee therefore instituted a policy of developing his country as the logistics hub of South-east Asia.

On taking office in 1961, Lee Kuan Yew set up the Economic Development Board (EDB), an organization that helped businesses to raise funds, manage finances, ensure security, issue shares, introduce technology, and so on. Later, with the establishment of banks, the financial responsibility of stock issuance and payment certification was transferred to them. Many state-run corporations separately bore responsibilities for other areas, including fund raising and management assistance. Nevertheless, economic planning and development remained firmly in the hands of the EDB. Lee shifted to a manufacturing-orientated policy and as a result, the manufacturing sector recorded an annual average growth of 23 per cent for the eight consecutive years from 1965. In particular, Singapore aggressively solicited foreign capital and as a result, in 1975, the proportion of businesses owned by foreigners amounted to 70 per cent of manufacturing production and 80 per cent of exports.

The proportion of Singapore's agriculture and forestry sector is a meagre 0.2 per cent, its manufacturing sector accounts for 26 per cent, but with 73.8 per cent, the service sector is the largest industry. Singapore attracts foreign businesses with its favourable investment climate, including its well-established infrastructure, thus boosting employment, securing a stable revenue source, and creating new investment and business opportunities. The proportion of the manufacturing sector in total exports was a mere 30 per cent in 1965 immediately after independence, but it soared to 60 per cent in 1975, and the average unemployment rate took a nosedive from 10 per cent to 2.7 per cent in 1995, resulting in a state of almost perfect employment. In 1973, 13 per cent of the total workforce was composed of foreigners because in addition to a general labour shortage, Singaporeans avoided 3D (difficult, dirty and dangerous) jobs. Furthermore, Singapore invited in hi-tech professionals from other countries so that it could overcome a chronic labour shortage and maintain world-class competitiveness.

More than anything, it is political stability that has supported Singaporean economic growth. PAP rule, uninterrupted since independence, has prevented the country from experiencing confusion from political power changes or wasting resources through frequent elections. However, it is true that Singapore is criticized at home and abroad for perpetuating a one-party dictatorship in the name of development. There is also scepticism about whether Singapore is capable of becoming a truly advanced country because it has no experience with democracy in the true sense of the term. But in the end, it is a decision that the Singaporeans will have to make for themselves.

Transparent administration

Singapore has been following and developing British-style administrative systems so effectively since the early stages of its national foundation that it now has the world's best administrative system. Government employees are the most respected in Singapore and comprise excellent-quality personnel. They are highly paid, treated exceptionally well, and their social status is higher than that of professors or executives of large corporations. However, if they abuse their power or engage in corrupt practices, they are punished severely. Despite having a relatively small number of government employees to carry out the volume of work, Singapore's government service is well-known for its transparency, efficiency and productivity. In some areas, it is rated higher than that of Japan.

Government employees provide a variety of services in order to attract foreign capital. For example, they provide one-stop services to companies, from initial set-up to the fully-operational stage. And they always think and act from an investor's point of view. In short, government employees are crucial factors behind Singapore's remarkable development. The lessons to be learnt from Singapore's example are as follows. The number of administrative bureaucrats should be dramatically reduced and the quality of personnel improved; a sufficient amount of pay should be guaranteed so that workers can concentrate on doing their jobs well; and government regulations should be removed through the introduction of a positive system.

System, the development engine

Singapore's economy has grown continuously at a rate of 8–9 per cent since its independence. The engine for such growth includes bold infrastructure investment, stable foreign capital inflow, and the power stemming from huge financial capital that the country enjoys as a world financial centre. First and foremost, however, it is the 'system power' created by the co-operation between the small but strong government and the flexible and effectively-managed substructure. In addition, the rate of women's economic participation, which has more than doubled, from a mere 21 per cent in the 1960s to 50 per cent in 1995, is higher than in the rest of the South-east Asian nations.

Potential and limits

Singapore is a city-state that can be compared to Venice, the past leader of trade in the Mediterranean. Singapore joined the NIC list in the 1970s and as a result of its continued high growth, its income level is among the highest in the world. However, despite huge reclamation projects, Singapore's land area totals a mere 646 km², (comparable to the size of Seoul, the capital of South Korea), and its population is just 3.1 million. Also, Singapore is a multi-ethnic state, with 78 per cent of the population of Chinese origin; 14 per cent of Malay origin, and 7 per cent of Indian origin, offering a high possibility of political and economic confusion. Worse still, the country lacks natural resources, and even water is provided by Malaysia. Also, having Indonesia with its huge population of 200 million nearby severely limits Singapore's political options. Moreover, since neighbouring countries are using Singapore as an exemplar, the country can no longer enjoy unchallenged superiority as it did in the past.

Though limited prosperity can be enjoyed, Singapore is too small to lead the regional economies. And though the country is making efforts to attract leading foreign corporations for industrial restructuring, neighbouring countries are competing to provide more favourable conditions, so it is questionable whether Singapore can offset quantitative shortages only by efficiency. Weakness with respect to technological development capacity and small domestic markets has led to an economic structure dependent on the production bases of foreign businesses and transit trade. Thus Singapore's economy is vulnerable to external changes, including strong challengers and international economic recession.

With a good understanding of such limitations, the Singaporean government aggressively encouraged the overseas expansion of domestic businesses up to the early 1990s. Since late 1992, however, the country has altered its strategy and encouraged the same companies to make intensive inroads into the neighbouring Asian region. According to the new strategy, Singapore is increasing investment in its Asian neighbours including China (investments amounted to US$1570m in 1996, making China the fifth largest) and India. If it maintains the strong points discussed earlier, Singapore will be able to further solidify its ground within the Asian economic bloc and continue to prosper.

Notes

1. Malacca: a small city located on a channel between Indonesia and Malaysia.
2. There is a similar organization in South Korea with the same name.

References

Chia Siow-Yue and Cheng, Bifan (1987) (Singapore: ISEAS) *ASEAN–China Economic Relations*
EIU (1997) *Singapore, The Economist*.
International Monetary Fund (1997) *Directory of Trade Statistics Yearbook*.
Mitsubishi Research Institute (1996) *Total Forecasting of Asia*
Pluvier, Jan (1974) *Southeast Asia from Colonialism to Independence* (Kuala Lumpur: Oxford University Press)

8
Overseas Chinese, the Catalyst for the Chinese Economic Sphere

The engine for pax-China

The latent energy and potential of the Chinese economy have been thrust into the limelight as the world turns its eyes toward Asia. What has taken the world by surprise at the same time, however, is the power of Chinese nationals scattered around the globe. Though they have different residences and nationalities, overseas Chinese are exerting overwhelming economic power through the so-called 'China networks' based on a sense of belonging and common experience. They dominate the South-east Asian economies, in particular, and on the basis of that are even exerting strong political power there.

In the case of Korea, because of its fundamental exclusionism toward foreigners, only 20 000 Chinese live there. In Japan, the number reaches 250 000, but their economic power is minimal. With the exception of these two countries, however, it is not an exaggeration to say that the economic strength of overseas Chinese in the whole of Asia is absolute. It was the overseas Chinese who empowered China to push forward with its economic development despite the USA's blockade policy.

Most overseas Chinese conglomerates[1] are pushing simultaneously for several giant projects in mainland China. They join hands with their counterparts rather than go it alone, making the most of economies of scale as well as reducing risks.[2]

In Japan, corporate research institutes are conducting in-depth studies of overseas Chinese, and Japanese businesses are utilizing the findings to make inroads into South-east Asian markets. Most South-east Asian nations ban foreigners from owning more than half of their real estate, and stocks and shares. Therefore, with local adaptation or market exploration, the possibility of success is improved if Japanese companies join hands with the Chinese residents rather than the local people. Furthermore, Chinese residents dominate the distribution networks with their unique business ability, and Japan possesses sophisticated technological and capital capacity. Accordingly, the reciprocal relationship between Japan and the overseas Chinese is expected to grow stronger. Since overseas Chinese are innately hard-working as well as having superior business ability and an international network, their influence is expected to grow further with the development of the Asian economies.

The profile of Overseas Chinese

The history of the migration of overseas Chinese dates back to the Tang dynasty at the end of the ninth century. Since they had been suffering from invasions by the non-Chinese tribes of the north, most of the Chinese people migrated to the south. At the time of the Mongol and Manchu invasions too, they moved *en masse* to the south. Since then, constant war and famine have driven the Chinese to settle in various countries world-wide. The number of Chinese residents scattered across the globe is estimated to be 56 million, 85 per cent of whom live in South-east Asia, with about 6 million in Hong Kong and Macao, and about 21 million in Taiwan.

The concentration of the population in South-east Asia is because the Chinese who went to Indonesia with the Yuan military expedition in the thirteenth century later remained there. Categorized more specifically, they can be divided into Huaqiao, those with Chinese or Taiwanese nationality, and Huaren, a second generation with local citizenship. They will collectively be referred to as 'Overseas Chinese' hereinafter. Overseas Chinese in South-east Asia hold estimated assets of about US$3 trillion, accounting for over 40 per cent of the total assets of South-east Asian nations. The total assets of the 1000 largest corporations listed in the top ten Asian stock markets amount to US$1140 billion, and about US$540 billion, which amounts to 42 per cent is owned by overseas Chinese.

Table 8.1   Migration history of Chinese residents in South-East Asia

Time	Region of migration	Background and process
1292	Indonesia, Java	After the Yuan military expedition failed, Chinese soldiers remained
13th–14th Centuries	Thailand	After the Yuan invasion of Thailand by the Sung dynasty, Chinese soldiers remained
15th Century	Malaysia	Chinese refugees who fled the Ming dynasty
17th–18th Centuries	Vietnam	Chinese refugees who fled the Ming dynasty stayed in Cochin-China
	Cambodia	Chinese residents in Vietnam and Vietnamese soldiers flowed in
After 18th Century	Thailand	Zheng Zhaow, of Chinese origin, founded the Bangkok dynasty
19th Century	Malaysia	Massive inflow of Chinese workers in the British colonial development zone
19th–20th Centuries	Indonesia	Massive inflow of Chinese workers in the Dutch colonial development zone

Source: Yi, Moon-bong (1995) *Overseas Chinese Business in Southeast Asia* (Korea: Gil-but Publishing Co.).

In most South-east Asian nations, half of the total workforce is employed by small and medium-sized enterprises, and 90 per cent of the SMEs are Chinese-owned. Accordingly, overseas Chinese are acting as the driving force of Asian economic development, based on their overwhelming economic power.

Overseas Chinese residents in Thailand number 5.57 million, a mere 10 per cent of the total population, but they own 60 per cent of the national wealth and 81 per cent of the total capital of listed businesses. In Indonesia, 5.81 million Overseas Chinese account for a mere 3.5 per cent of the total population but own 73 per cent of the listed businesses and 50 per cent of the national wealth. Singapore is a truly an Overseas Chinese country, with the Chinese population accounting for 77 per cent of the total and owning 81 per cent of the total capital. The top ten conglomerates in Indonesia, nine out of ten in Thailand; five out of six in Singapore, four in the Philippines, and three in Malaysia are owned by Overseas Chinese residents. In Malaysia, 29 per cent of Overseas Chinese have control of 61 per cent of the listed corporations and 50 per cent of the national wealth. In the Philippines, with a mere 2 per cent of the total population, they dominate 50 per cent of listed corporations and 60 per cent of natural wealth, respectively. Thus, it is not an overstatement to say that South-east Asian economies are in the hands of Overseas Chinese. Furthermore, in the USA, more than a million Overseas Chinese are living in California alone, and a considerable number are living in Canada and Australia as well, constructing worldwide networks.

If these Overseas Chinese were considered to be one economic group, they would be third only to the USA and Japan in terms of economic power.[3] These Overseas Chinese are making massive investments in China. According to statistics for the end of 1993, among the ten largest investing nations in China, Singapore and Thailand ranked sixth and ninth, respectively. While this does not seem significant on the surface, considering that a huge amount of investment by Hong Kong, the biggest investor in China, is made by Overseas Chinese corporations operating in ASEAN, actual investments made by Overseas Chinese are increased dramatically. This is because it is the strategy of most Overseas Chinese businesses operating in ASEAN to establish

Table 8.2   Numbers of Chinese residents in ASEAN and their capital, 1991

	Singapore	Malaysia	Thailand	The Philippines	Indonesia	Total
Total number of residents	214	533	557	120	581	2 005
Place of origin						
Fujian	86	171	56	102	290	705
Guangdong	39	117	39	14	192	401
Huzhou	49	59	312	0	0	420
Hakan	19	128	89	0	93	329
Hainan	15	21	50	0	0	86
Other	6	37	11	4	6	64
Chinese residents/total population (%)	77	29	10	2	3.5	121.5
Capital owned by Chinese residents/total capital (%)[1]	81	61	81	50	73	69.2

Note: [1] Proportions in aggregate value of listed stocks, except for government and foreign capital.
Source: Yamaguchi, Seisho (1993) 'The Era of Overseas Chinese Economic Sphere', *Estimation of Business*, vol. 4.

subsidiaries in Hong Kong and make inroads into China through such subsidiaries.

Such Overseas Chinese investment in China made through Hong Kong accounted for 80 per cent of total foreign direct investment. Nevertheless, the USA and Japan were not aware of this before the Tiananmen Square incident. After this incident, the USA tried to force concessions from China on its human rights record by withholding funds to the country. However, the USA belatedly came to realize the existence of powerful Overseas Chinese in the background.

Because Japan engaged in detour exports through production bases in South-east Asia to avoid import restrictions by advanced countries in the West, the priority markets of Japan, its economic role there gradually increased. The reason South-east Asia is able to lead the global economic development of the 1990s is mainly attributable to Japan. When Japan moved its production bases to South-east Asia, it also spread its capital and expertise. However, encouraged by this success, Japan became overconfident of its importance and was not aware of the formidable power of the Overseas Chinese until Tiananmen Square.

This power of the Overseas Chinese had been developed during a long process of national energy accumulation. The Han, who had escaped to the south from the Mongol invasion in the thirteenth century had little to do but engage in money-making businesses. The only possibilities open to them were economic activities, so while at first they were engaged in agriculture, they founded small household industries and sold their products through nationwide merchant networks. The networks were dominated by Xiangfang, an organization made up of Chinese with similar origins. Xiangfangs, which were established across the nation, formed an organization to collect and distribute goods made by household manufacturers, and such networks expanded as the Overseas Chinese scattered across the world. China utilizes these Overseas Chinese networks to introduce capital and expertise in addition to boosting exports. The Tiananmen Square incident proved that as long as China has such lines of communication, the USA cannot control the Chinese economy at will. The Chinese economy is therefore expected to form a far bigger sphere through its overseas Chinese networks in the foreseeable future.

The Kejiawu, 'The Jews of Asia'

The Kejiawu[4] are unique and they must be mentioned when discussing Overseas Chinese. They are those who fled from the Northern Song to the Southern Song at the time of the Mongol invasion in the thirteenth century. When they moved to the south, the fertile lands of the south was already occupied by settlers, so the Kejiawus were relegated to living in remote areas. Living together in Guangdong, Fujian and Jiangxi, they mostly made a living working as low-grade government officials or businessmen. There are about 45 million living in mainland China and about 5 million in the South-east Asian region, with a majority of them concentrated in Thailand, Indonesia and Taiwan. Since they have survived only through their ability and hard work, the Kejiawus have a particularly wise outlook on life and excellent business skills, placing them at the centre of the Overseas Chinese. Overseas Chinese residents in South-east Asia total 21 million, a mere 6 per cent of the total population, but they own 40 per cent of the total capital, controlling the region's commerce. Among these Overseas Chinese, the Kejiawus, a minority, are at the top and their importance within the future Chinese economic sphere is expected to grow stronger.

The future prospects for Overseas Chinese

It was their overwhelming economic power that made the world pay attention to Overseas Chinese, products of a dark history of migration. Furthermore, their commitment to the construction of New Asia, a giant economic bloc, is anticipated because of the synergy that their world-wide networks and their economic power will create. Nevertheless, if their power is misused for the construction of a Chinese-centred world, Overseas Chinese will face strong resistance from local residents of the countries they reside in.

Even a protective shield of overwhelming economic power is useless before a political revolution that accompanies a changed sentiment of the people. Taiwan, even though established as a state, is being deprived of its local property by China because of its reduced political status. This indicates clearly what kind of situation the Overseas Chinese, a political minority, will face in the worst-case scenario. Overseas Chinese will therefore be able to strengthen their position within the region only when they work as a strong force to unite New Asia based on their understanding of the local culture and economy.

Notes

1. Representative overseas Chinese conglomerates include Liemshiwei Ion of Indonesia (US$3bn property); Robert Kuok of Malaysia (US$2.1bn property); Likashing of Hong Kong (UK$5.8bn property); Danin Chearabanont of Thailand (UK$5.3bn property); and Quack Jebeng of Singapore (US$5bn property).
2. Of the (US$179 30 million of foreign capital investments in China during 1979–91, 66.7 per cent was overseas Chinese capital from Hong Kong, Macao, Taiwan so on.
3. The World Bank expects that the Chinese economic sphere, including China (Hong Kong included) and Taiwan will emerge as the largest world-wide by 2002, with an economic scale of US$9800 billion.
4. They are called 'Kejiawu' in Mandarin and 'Haka' in Hakan. A considerable number (45 million currently living in China and 5 million in Southeast Asia but they account for a tiny 4 per cent because of the huge Chinese population. They are often likened to Jews because they have produced many prominent figures in spite of their small population. Representative figures of Hakan origin include Zhu-zi, the originator of Zhu-zi Theory; Wang Yangming, the founder of the doctrines of Wang Yangming; Sun Yat-sen, the originator of the Threefold National Principle; Hong Xiuquan, the initiator of the Taiping Rebellion; Deng Xiaoping, China's Number One man; Lee Deng Hui, prime minister of Taiwan; and Lee Kuan Yew, the former premier and 'father' of Singapore. Kejiawus are characterized by their thorough realism – placing great importance on reality without being swayed by ideology. Of world-wide Overseas Chinese businesses, the top twenty in sales are of Kejiawu origin, proving how powerful they are in the Overseas Chinese community.

References

The Economist Intelligence Unit (1997) *China, The Economist*
General Agreement on Tariffs and Trade, International Trade
Kim Hi-ju and Hong Suk-il (1995) *Challenges of ASEAN* (Korea: KIET)
League of Nations (1995) *Statistical Yearbook of the League of Nations*
Robert Lloyd George (1992) *The East-West Pendulum* (Simon & Schuster).
Park Jung-dong (1995) 'One China', *The Korea Economic Daily.*
Yi, Moor-bong (1995) *Overseas Chinese Businesses in Southeast Asia* (Korea: Gil-but Publishing Co.).

9
New Members of New Asia

Australia

Australia was a colony of Britain for a long time. Based on its special relationship with Britain after its independence and with the USA after the Second World War, it upheld the idea of 'White Australianism'.[1] As a result, Australia was labelled one of the most racist countries in the world. However, Australia later became aware of global trends and abandoned its racist policy in 1973.

Australia maintained its ANZUS[2] Pact with the USA and New Zealand from 1951, but just as trust among the signatories was weakening, New Zealand's refusal to allow US nuclear submarines to call at its ports resulted in the country's expulsion in 1985. Since then, Australia maintained its relationship with the USA. Despite its adherence to White Australianism, Australia has always been at the forefront of Asia's history. During the Second World War, when Japanese forces reached Papua New Guinea, Australia entered the war alongside the Allies. The country also actively participated in the Korean War and the Vietnam War. Nevertheless, Australia did so only to protect its interests in Asia and not because it considered itself to be a member of the region. Entering the 1980s, however, Australia's view on Asia began to change gradually, for the following reasons.

First, the defeat of the USA in the Vietnam War revealed the limits of US power and determination. Moreover, as a country upholding multiracialism, the USA had no cause to protect the racist Australia from neighbouring countries. Another factor for change that cannot be ignored is the strengthened political and economic power of Asia

Table 9.1   Changes in US immigrants

Place of origin	1900–20	1981–85
North-western Europe	34	6
South-western Europe	41	8
North America	10	2
Asia	5	42
South America	6	36
Other	4	6

Note: 2.4 million illegal immigrants have been excluded.
Source: *US Immigration Office Statistics Yearbook* (1986).

which gave more organized power to criticisms about White Australianism. Since the 1980s, scepticism about the ANZUS alliance has surfaced. As a consequence, it was widely agreed that Australia should develop Asianized political and economic strategies instead of depending on the USA.

Second, the active acceptance of immigrants of Asian origin contributed a great deal to the national development of the US and Canada. After 1967, the US revised its immigration policy and widely accepted immigrants from Asia; of the total immigrants during 1981–5, 42 per cent were of Asian origin. As these immigrants helped to make the US economy more robust, and as Canada cultivated its national power in the same way, Australia could no longer afford the disadvantages stemming from its adherence to the anachronistic White Australianism.[3]

Third, Australia grew far more dependent on Asia than on the EU in terms of trade. In 1996, 64.9 per cent of Australia's exports and 41.1 per cent of its imports were dependent on Asian countries. As can be seen from Table 9.2, South Korea (9.4 per cent) surpasses the USA (6.3 per cent) and is second only to Japan (19.7 per cent) in market size. In the meantime, the EU's share has gradually been reduced, to 10.8 per cent in 1996. What is notable here is that the UK proportion, Australia's mother nation, stood at a mere 3.5 per cent, lower even than those of Singapore (3.7 per cent), Indonesia (4 per cent), and Hong Kong (3.8 per cent).

Australia is a continent-state with a vast land area of 7.68 million km^2, similar to the size of the continental USA (excluding Alaska), but it is sparsely populated, with only 18.3 million residents. On the

Table 9.2 Import–export dependency on Australia, mid-1996

Place of origin	Export dependency (%)	Import dependency (%)
Japan	19.7	13
South Korea	9.4	3
New Asia	64.9	41.1
EU (excl. UK)	10.8	24.9
USA	6.3	23.4
UK	3.5	6.4

Source: The Economist Intelligence Unit (1999) *Australia*.

Table 9.3 Australia's major economic indicators

	1992	1994	1996
Population (millions)	17.4	17.8	18.3
Gross domestic product (US$ billions)	293.9	324.1	389.8
Consumer price rate of increase (%)	1.0	1.9	2.6
Exports (US$ billions)	42.8	47.3	59.8
Imports (US$ billions)	41.2	50.6	60.5
GDP growth rate (%)	2.8	5.0	4.3
Total foreign debts (US$ billions)	143.2	150.1	174.4

Source: The Economist Intelligence Unit (1997) *Australia*.

world map, the Australian continent, with the lowest population density, lies to the south of the densely populated Asia. This indicates the possibility of future co-prosperity between Australia, with its abundant natural resources, and Asia, with its huge human resources.

As can be seen from Table 9.4, the GDP of Australia can be broken down according to its economic activities, as follows. Of the total US$392 billion, the proportions of primary industries, including agriculture and mining, and tertiary industries are 8.4 per cent and 74.5 per cent respectively, higher than those of major advanced countries. The manufacturing sector accounts for a mere 17.1 per cent, showing its limit to continuous economic development.[4] In particular, it can be said that Australia survives because of its 800 000 miners since its dependency on the mining industry is so high. As can be seen in Table 9.5, of total exports amounting to US$59.9 billion, minerals and metals are worth US$14.2 billion, coal

Table 9.4 Proportions of Australia's economic activities in GDP

Industry	Proportion
Primary industry	8.4
Manufacturing	17.1
Construction	6.4
Transportation & communications	9.7
Public administration	3.6
Other	54.8

Source: The Economist Intelligence Unit (1997) *Australia.*

and petroleum, US$9.4 billion, and gold, US$4.9 billion. In total, minerals account for half of the entire export volume. Australia is a continent rich in mineral resources.[5] It has many open-cast mines and because the quality of the minerals is good, most Asian countries import large quantities from Australia.[6] On the other hand, wool, despite being closely associated with Australia, accounts for only US$3.7 billion, and cereals a mere US$3.7 billion. As such, the proportion of agriculture is relatively small compared to the size of the land area.

In terms of GDP breakdown, in 1995 exports represented about 19.6 per cent; investments, 21.3 per cent; and government consumption, 17.5 per cent. Although the ratios of exports and investments are low, private consumption accounted for 62.5 per cent. Australia has a structure where consumption exceeds production. That is why the country's economic achievement is low despite its huge potential for economic development. Also, the structure of the manufacturing sector lags behind other countries, with 15 per cent in agricultural product processing, 6 per cent in textiles, and 20 per cent in machinery. This is because Australia has funnelled foreign currency, earned by exporting minerals and agricultural products, into uncompetitive import-substitution industries. Australia's domestic manufacturing industries are import-substitution-orientated, thereby weakening its international competitiveness. Because Australia cannot export its produced goods, which lack international competitiveness, these products are sold in the domestic markets at high prices, perpetuating a vicious circle that burdens the national economy.

Table 9.5   Australia's major exports

Exports	Amount (US$ bn)
Minerals and metals	14.2
Coal and petroleum	9.4
Machinery	7.6
Gold	4.9
Cereals	3.7
Other	20.1
Total	59.9

Source: International Monetary Fund, *Directory of Trade Statistics* (1997).

Recently, along with market opening, Australia has abandoned the uncompetitive manufacturing sector and concentrated on fostering priority industries. Through the process of actively pursuing economic efficiency Australia has further strengthened its relationship with Asia. A trade agreement signed with Japan in 1957 placed the country at the top of Australia's exporting partners list.[7] Recently, however, to reduce excessive dependency on Japan, Australia is trying to diversify its trade into New Asian nations including South Korea, China and Singapore.

Trade dependency alone clearly indicates the direction Australia's national strategy should take. With regard to imports, Australia is still highly dependent on Asia, with 41.1 per cent of total imports coming from that region. The reason Australia has an excessive foreign debt of US$174.4 billion is because state management has been inefficient despite abundant natural resources and a vast land area.

As can be seen in Table 9.6, after White Australianism was abandoned, Asians comprised 37.1 per cent of the 120 000 annual average of immigrants in the 1990s. Nevertheless, Asians number only 700 000, a mere 4 per cent of the total population.[8] Even if the trend of increasing Asian immigration continues, it will take a long time for the population structure to be altered. Another crucial factor that bars Australia from opening is the problem of national consciousness. Relations between groups can move on to a final level of reconciliation and co-operation only after going through stages of indifference and conflict. The relationship between Australia and Asia has just moved out of the stage of indifference.

Table 9.6   Australian Immigration

Country	1987 %	1990 %	1992 %
Hong Kong	3.3	8.7	10.4
Vietnam	4.9	11.3	7.8
New Zealand	12.0	7.4	7.8
India	2.2	3.1	5.4
The Philippines	7.0	5.1	5.2
China	2.4	2.7	3.6
Taiwan	0.8	2.6	2.4
Malaysia	4.0	5.1	2.3
Proportion of Asian immigrants	36.6	46.0	37.1
Total number of immigrants	128 290	121 560	94 250

Source: Foreign Policy Research Institute of Korea (1995) *Year Book Australia.*

In the late 1990s, dramatic increases in numbers of Asian immigrants are stirring up anti-Asian sentiments among Australians. However, because more than half of world trade is being conducted in the Asia-Pacific region, and considering Australia's geographical proximity to and economic dependency on the region, the resurgence of White Australianism, much reported by the local press, is likely to be reduced to groundless fear. The Australian government so far has shown considerable commitment to the formation and development of the Asia Pacific Economic Co-operation organization (APEC) – Australia took the lead in the founding of the APEC in 1989. However, a policy alienated from public opinion can rarely work. First and foremost, therefore, Australia should establish new values and seek a national consensus.

In addition to having a favourable climate, including abundant natural resources and vast land area, Australia has a good education system, with a college attendance rate of 40 per cent; 5.7 per cent of GDP is invested in education, thereby producing a high quality workforce. If Asia's excellent human resources and economic dynamics are incorporated, Australia will be able to emerge as a new power in the twenty-first century.

New Zealand

The population structure of New Zealand is similar to that of Australia, with Europeans accounting for 88 per cent and the 3000 00 aboriginal Maoris occupying 9 per cent. The expedition led by the Dutch navigator Abel Tasman attempted to land in New Zealand in 1642, but was repelled by the Maoris, and an attempt by an English expedition led by James Cook in 1769 was also repulsed by the well-organized Maoris. In 1840, Great Britain signed the Treaty of Waitangi with the Maoris. According to the Treaty, the Maoris ceded sovereignty to Britain on condition that Britain provided protection and recognized their land ownership. In the end, however, the Maoris ended up losing most of their land to the British.

A large number of both the aborigines in Australia and the Maori people in New Zealand have perished from the European-transmitted diseases. Even diseases that were not considered to be harmful to Europeans were deadly to the natives who had lived in total isolation for a long time and hence, lacked the immunity to resist them. However, the main cause of the dramatic decrease in the Maori population was the slaughter of the natives and disruption of their way of life by the Europeans in order to seize as much land as possible.

New Zealand occupies an area of 270 000 km^2, similar in size to Britain and Japan, but it has a small population of 3.62 million and a GDP of US$63.9 billion. In terms of New Zealand's economic structure, the manufacturing sector accounts for only 18.5 per cent,[9] and because its domestic market is small, its rate of trade dependency is a high 44 per cent. In this respect, the country's economic structure is even weaker than Australia's. As can be seen from Table 9.8, when expenditure in relation to GDP is considered, 15 per cent is in public spending and 64.2 per cent in private spending. In order to maintain high growth, investment needs to be maintained at a 30–40 per cent level, but in the case of New Zealand, it is only 22 per cent. In this context, Australia and New Zealand have less potential for growth compared to other Asian nations. Education in New Zealand accounted for 4.9 per cent of GDP in 1994, and the college attendance rate of those in the proper age group is 59.8 per cent.

Table 9.7   New Zealand's major economic indicators

	1992	*1996*
Population (millions)	3.44	3.62
Land size (000s km^2)	271	271
Gross national product (US$ billions)	39.4	63.9
Foreign reserves (US$ billions)	3.06	5.96
Foreign debt (US$ billions)	35.8	56.4
Real GDP growth rate (%)	2.2	1.9

Source: The Economist Intelligence Unit (1997) *New Zealand.*

Table 9.8   Expenditure to gross domestic product (percentages)

Private spending	*Public spending*	*Total capital formation*	*Exports*	*Imports*
64.2	15.0	21.6	32.8	–34.1

Source: The Economist Intelligence Unit (1997) *New Zealand.*

Among New Zealand's major exports, dairy products account for US$1.8 billion; meat, US$1.6 billion; timber, US$1.7 billion; wool, US$800 million; fisheries, US$500 million; and fruit and vegetables, US$800 million, all of which in total represent half of the total export amount of US$14.3 billion. Among its exporting partners, Australia takes 20.4 per cent and Japan, 15.4 per cent, making New Zealand less dependent on Asia for exports compared to Australia. However, considering the fact that two-thirds of Australia's trade is dependent on Asia, New Zealand's economy does not differ much from that of Australia.[10] Regarding imports, of the total amount of US$14.7 billion, Australia accounts for 24.2 per cent; the USA, 16.7 per cent and Japan, 14.3 per cent, while the rest is mainly from Asian countries.

Before the Second World War, New Zealand's economy depended on Britain for 80 per cent of its exports, but at the time of writing these stand at only 6.4 per cent. On the other hand, the proportion of the thirteen nations of New Asia is increasing. Accordingly, New Zealand is expected ultimately to declare itself a member of New Asia. New Zealand, through its 'Asia 2000' policy aimed at strengthening

Table 9.9   New Zealand's major trade partners (percentages)

Nation	Exports (%)	Imports (%)
Australia	20.4	24.2
Japan	15.4	14.3
USA	9.1	16.7
UK	6.4	5.2
China	2.6	3.7
South Korea	4.7	1.8
EU	4.5	20.2

Source: International Monetary Fund (1997) *Directory of Trade Statistics Yearbook.*

regional economic relations with New Asia, is trying to secure its position as a supply base for agricultural products and livestock for Asia. In particular, as the establishment of the WTO greatly expanded the market for agricultural products and livestock and also reduced tariffs, New Zealand is showing strong enthusiasm for advancing into Asian markets.

Like Australia, which in the past adhered to a whites-only immigration policy, New Zealand at first held Asia in check with the help of the USA. With the strengthening of Asia, however, New Zealand is increasingly trying to establish closer relationships with its neighbours in Asia. Most of the country's early immigrants were of European origin, but as in Australia, Asian immigrants are now increasing. Among the 54 800 immigrants admitted in 1995, 60 per cent were of Asian origin. Nevertheless, because cultural differences are expected to cause considerable conflict between the two groups, in order that the government and citizens of New Zealand can truly be reborn as an integral part of Asia, extraordinary efforts must be made by both parties.

Notes

1. White Australianism: Australia's white-first-policy of excluding the immigration of coloured people. After the adoption of the unified immigration restriction law in 1901, it was annulled in principle.
2. Indefinite collective security treaty signed between Australia, New Zealand and the USA in September, 1951.
3. After the abolition of White Australianism, immigration increased, from 0.58 per cent in 1972 to 0.86 per cent in 1982, but has shown a

downward movement since 1990 (0.74 per cent in 1990 and 0.2 per cent in 1993).

4. Regarding the proportion of primary industries, France recorded 2 per cent; Germany, 1 per cent; Italy, 3 per cent; Britain, 3 per cent; the US, 2 per cent; and Japan, 2 per cent. The proportion of manufacturing is over 20 per cent in most of these countries.

5. Australia is the world's biggest producer of bauxite, zircons and diamonds; the second in iron ores; and the third in nickel and zinc. In terms of deposits, bauxite has 39 per cent of the world's total, and coal, 2 per cent. (*Source*: Research Institute of Foreign Economies (1996) *Australia Handbook*, vol. 9).

6. In the case of coal, in 1993, New Asia (ten member nations) took 76.5 per cent; Europe, 14.6 per cent; and Africa and the Middle East, 3.2 per cent, respectively.

7. Australia depends greatly on Japan for exports because Japan imports and refines raw materials such as coal and iron ores using a long-term supply method (75 per cent of iron ores and 69 per cent of coal were exported to Japan in 1994).

8. Population is comprised of European whites (89.2 per cent); Asians (4.1 per cent); Arabs (1 per cent); and Aborigines (16 per cent). The white-dominated population structure resulted from the gold rush and 160 000 British prisoners banished there in the eighteenth century.

9. In addition, agriculture, forestry, fisheries and mining take 8 per cent each; construction, 2.8 per cent; transportation and communications, 10.9 per cent; and banking and industrial services, 10.6 per cent respectively – which shows the high proportion of the service industries.

10. The signing of the Closer Economic Agreement (CER) with Australia in the manufacturing industries further activated the bilateral exchange.

10
India: Another Asian Giant

To attempt to define India and its 950 million people in a few words would be as difficult as a blind person describing an elephant. India, with its vast land area, is the birthplace of Buddhism and Hinduism, and its people have constructed a profoundly spiritual civilization. Although part of it is crumbling, the caste system is still strictly maintained, and 1652 languages and 190 religions coexist in this land where artificial satellites are designed and hi-tech software is produced. The gap between the rich and the poor is so extreme that 52 per cent of the population earn less than one US dollar a day. As a formidable military power with nuclear weapons, it was the leader of the Third World for about four decades. These are the mysteries of India.

Although it has been fifty years since its independence in 1947 from 190 years of British colonial rule, only a few years have passed since India adopted a free economic system and launched full-scale development.[1] As the Indian economy began to lag behind China's, a rival it once went to war with, the Rao regime overhauled the existing economic policy and formulated a new one based on 'economic liberalization and opening'.[2] In line with this new policy, the regime abolished the Swadeshi (self-support) economy with its strong socialistic elements, privatized public businesses, and attracted foreign capital aggressively.

The motives behind such economic reforms in India are – political shock from the collapse of the USSR; the economic reforms of Pakistan and China, India's rival countries; a sense of crisis stemming from the high economic growth of South-east Asian nations;

and intensified conflicts among various religions and classes. With the revolutionary measures implemented in 1991 India accomplished a remarkable success and the Gowda administration that took office in June 1996 is following the same economic reform policy. In this chapter, I attempt to explain why India, with such diversity and potential, is categorized as an Asian nation, by reviewing its cultural and historical background, and further, attempt to forecast its future.

A country, far yet near

India is naturally categorized as an Asian nation when its history and culture are taken into account, while from an economic point of view it is less close to Asia than are Australia or New Zealand. Nevertheless, as the birthplace of Buddhism, one of Asia's biggest religions, India has been interacting with Asia for 2500 years, thus greatly affecting the development of Asia. Most Buddhist terminology, in particular, originated from the Sanskrit language and has been localized in various nations after years of usage. Even though India has been a Hindu nation since the thirteenth century, because Hinduism evolved from the same native religion as Buddhism, Asia and India have much in common. Also, due to its continuous contact with Asia through the Silk Road or maritime trade, India is emotionally close to Asia.

Some ten million Indian nationals are living scattered around the globe, with a total income amounting to US$340 billion, an amount that almost equals the GDP of India. These Indian nationals will rise as a new power in the twenty-first century after forming a network linking Singapore, Hong Kong, the USA, the UK and South Africa. Indians living in South-east Asia, in particular, have built up considerable political power. As a result, they are expected to contribute greatly to solidifying the framework of New Asia.

Twin pillars of Asia

India's role is crucial to Asia's balanced development in the future. This is because no one can entirely rule out the possibility that China, with its 1.2 billion population, will resort to military hegemony, propelled by its explosive economic growth. Therefore, the role of India as a restraining influence to keep China in check and maintain the power balance within Asia is emphasized. The US is actively supporting India's membership in APEC as a way to groom that country into a force that could counter the ever-growing influence of China.

If one expands this logic to the level of a world power structure, the role of India becomes more significant. Since the collapse of Communism terminated ideological conflicts, countries have entered into infinite competition for economic power. World economies are showing a contradictory picture of simultaneously increasing globalization and localization. Under the circumstances, India is expected to keep in balance with China within Asia while contributing to Asia's pursuit of open regionalism on an equal footing with the USA and the EU.

The birth of a unified India

India is too small to be a continent, but at the same time it is too large for a single central government to maintain complete control over it. This would have been particularly true in the past when communication and transportation means were not well developed. For these reasons, until the British rule, India was never a unified country in the truest sense of the word.

The Narmada river that runs east to west along the middle divides India into northern and southern parts. The country is blocked by the Himalayas to the north and by mountains along its border with Myanmar to the east. Therefore, war and cultural exchanges have mainly taken place in the north-west, which is relatively open in terms of geography. At one time India was under pressure from three forces at the same time: from the north-west, Afghanistan and Kazakstan, a Central Asian country; from the east, Myanmar and Bangladesh; and from the south, southern India. None of these forces, however, was strong enough to conquer the whole subcontinent.

Around the sixth century kingdoms, including Mahad and Kosala, were founded. In 317 BC, the Maurya dynasty was founded, developing into a relatively well-established and unified state, but it is difficult to consider this as complete unification. However, during the three-centuries-long prosperity of this dynasty, Buddhist culture blossomed and spread throughout Asia. For about five centuries

159

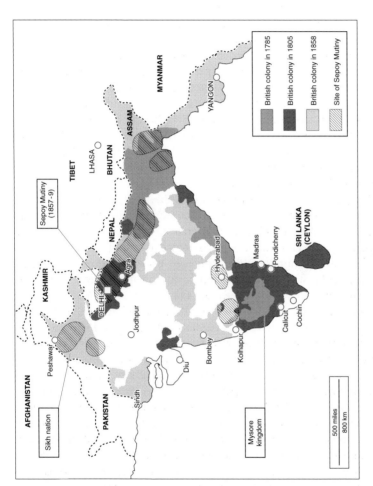

Map 10.1   Power in India at the time of the British invasion

afterwards, however, the dynasty faced repeated divisions and incessant wars. During the fourth century AD, the Gupta empire was founded and ruled northern India, whereas southern India was divided into many different kingdoms. The Gupta empire was not able to extend its power to southern India. Around this time, Hinduism replaced Buddhism and strengthened its position based on native religions. Around the eleventh century AD, however, the Ghazni dynasty was founded following an Afghanistan invasion. Foreign invasions continued, and Islam was introduced in the thirteenth century. With the introduction of Islam, kingdoms like Silvi, Tughluq, Vidianna and Lodi were founded, resulting in Islamic settlements in the north-west. Around 1526, the Mughal empire was established and, based in northern India, it ruled for about 150 years, but it collapsed after being defeated by foreign forces from Afghanistan and, in the midst of the confusion that followed, Great Britain advanced into Bengal.

Bengal, a north-eastern region of India, was chosen as a base by Britain since western India was already occupied by Portugal, Holland and France. After that Britain mustered scattered feudal lords through stratagem and continuous war, thereby expanding its power. Britain was able to dominate India with ease because the power struggle within India was directly related to the power struggle in Europe. Britain, which had overpowered The Netherlands and France in Europe, expelled French, Dutch and Portuguese forces from India.

Even though there were numerous feudal lords and kings in India, because they were hostile toward each other they found themselves under the control of Britain which carried out elaborate century-long colonization strategies. Britain repeatedly helped or joined hands with one of two confronting lords in order to overpower the other and absorb his kingdom. In this way Britain finally dominated the whole subcontinent. Ironically, unification, which no one had accomplished throughout India's long history, was ultimately realized by a foreign force which deprived the nation of its sovereignty. It is similar to the case of China, which paradoxically expanded its borders when placed under foreign control during the Yuan and Qing dynasty.

However, Indians gained a sense of unity through a rebellion started by sepoy, mercenaries of Britain, in 1857. In fact, Asians themselves have never had a sense of being in 'Asia'. Asia was defined by

Europeans, and European oppression and exploitation engendered a sense of unity among Asians, resulting in the Asian identity. In the same vein, since each region had been living independently for thousands of years with different languages and blood lineages, Indians lacked a sense of psychological homogeneity as a nation. Hostility against Britain along with a burgeoning sense of a shared common fate as oppressed people led to rebellion. Any rebellion was quickly subdued, however, because it was without a centripetal point and was unable to challenge Britain in an organized way.

The East India Company, which ruled India, accumulated an astronomical amount of wealth in the course of selling taxation rights to Indians, which enabled it to further build up its power, even in Britain. As corruption and irregularities became serious problems, the British government abolished the company in 1858 and assumed direct control of India. The sepoy rebellion, while ending in failure, led to the rise of a national consciousness and the founding of the Indian National Congress in 1885. The Congress, however, failed to overcome religious barriers, causing followers of Islam to break away in 1905 to establish the Islamic Federation. When the First World War broke out soon afterwards, many Indian soldiers took part, and taxes were used to support the war. Nevertheless, after the war, Britain betrayed India and committed a mass slaying of Indians in the Amritsar Massacre in 1919. Indians continued systematic and non-violent resistance under the leadership of Mahatma Gandhi, who gave Indians an unprecedented sense of identity before the country finally achieved independence.

Remarkable potential

India's GDP is only US$328.4 billion, but this is just nominal income. According to a recent analysis by the World Bank, India's GDP according to purchasing power valuation is estimated to be far greater, reaching about US$1 trillion. First the economy of scale alone with a population of 950 million is very large.

In particular, a fifth of the population, amounting to about 120 million people, is middle-class, with considerable purchasing power, giving Indian markets huge potential. With respect to the GDP of 1995, 27.9 per cent was agriculture, while a mere 19.7 per cent was manufacturing. Also, 8.9 per cent was exports; 6.8 per cent imports;

Table 10.1   India's major economic indicators

	1992	1994	1996*
Population (millions)	867.8	935.7	954.5
Gross domestic product (US$ billions)	235.5	328.4	330.7
Exports (US$ billions)	18.5	31.8	33.1
Imports (US$ billions)	21.9	36.7	38.5
Foreign reserves (US$ billions) (exluding gold)	5.8	17.9	20.2
Total foreign debts (US$ billions)	89.8	94.3	93.2
GDP growth rate (%)	5.3	5.3	6.8

Note: * Estimate.
Source: The Economist Intelligence Unit (1997) 'India', *The Economist.*

and 26 per cent investment. As seen in the breakdown, investment levels are too low and trade dependency has declined too much as a result of concentrating on import-substitution industries targeting domestic markets.

Among the total export amount of US$31.8 billion in 1995, jewellery accounted for US$5.3 billion; clothes, US$3.7 billion; textiles, US$2.6 billion; and leather, US$1.7 billion. Half of total exports were composed of low value-added products, showing a structural weakness of the economy. Among exporting partners of 1996, the USA accounted for 17 per cent, Germany, 6.9 per cent, Japan, 7.3 per cent, and Britain, 6.6 per cent. Hence India is highly dependent on the West and its export dependency on Middle Eastern countries is also high, recording 8.5 per cent.

In case of importing partners, the USA accounted for 9.1 per cent; the EU, 30.4 per cent; the Middle East, 15.9 per cent; and Japan, 6.6 per cent – also resulting in high dependency on the West. The rest of the Asian nations have minimal import and export transactions with India. However, in terms of the total scale of the New Asia this book proposes, India's dependency on New Asia will be 29.3 per cent for exports and 27.4 per cent for imports. In securing funds for economic development, since the economic liberalization in 1991, India has reversed its policy from dependence on foreign aid and loans to actively attracting foreign investment. As a result, India attracted about US$10 billion foreign investment (based on approved amount) for the period 1991 to February 1995. Among the investors, the USA tops the list, followed by Britain, Japan and Germany, in that order.

Table 10.2   India's major trading partners (percentages)

Country	Export %	Import %
USA	17.0	9.1
Germany	6.9	8.4
UK	6.6	7.0
Middle East	8.5	15.9
EU	27.0	30.4
New Asia	29.3	27.4
Japan	7.3	6.6
Hong Kong	5.2	2.0
Singapore	2.2	4.5

Source: International Monetary Fund (1997) *Directory of Trade Statistics Yearbook.*

In particular, India is liberalizing investments in virtually all fields except security-related fields such as national defence and nuclear power, and those related to health and safety. Most foreign investments are concentrated in the fields of oil refining, electricity, electronics, communications, chemicals, and industrial equipment.[3]

India's investment in education is a mere 3.5 per cent of GDP, and the college attendance rate is 44 per cent. Nevertheless, India has more abundant high-quality human resources than any other country.[4] India's population breakdown is as follows: 71 per cent Aryans; 25 per cent Dravidians; and 3 per cent Mongoloids, mainly living in eastern India, including the Asem region. India is an important region in that it is racially between Asia and Europe, and functioning as a religious buffer zone between Islam and Buddhism.

Backward administration and widespread corruption

The biggest vices of the Indian economy are corruption, backwardness and inefficiency of government employees; vices that have been accumulating for half a century. The Indian government carries out regulation-orientated policies, thereby inevitably incurring inefficiency. Even the scale of production units is decided by government employees, for example. Influenced by socialist economics, India made most of its major key industries public. As low productivity accompanied deficits, India is irrationally trying to maintain a monopoly system by acquiring even competitive private businesses in order to survive. A series of measures going against economic common sense greatly weakened the national competitiveness of India. According to recent statistics, 102 out of 236 public companies are in the red, and the rest are making a profit by shifting responsibility for the inefficient and high cost management to consumers by using their monopolistic status. The most urgent issue, therefore, for Indian economic development, is the privatization of public enterprises.[5]

The existing public companies are so inefficient and employees so powerful that private companies are not interested in acquiring these businesses. Therefore, to improve efficiency while minimizing the national burden, India should move toward liberalization by actively encouraging private companies that are in competition with public enterprises. Since public companies at the time of writing account for 27 per cent of the employed population, 62 per cent of invested capital and 30 per cent of value added, if the inefficiency of public companies goes uncorrected, the possibility of the Indian economy recovering its competitiveness is remote.

Every business is corrupt, from top to bottom, and the management itself is crude and technically backward. Even worse, power struggles are so widespread that many businesses are being run with the CEO position unfilled. Therefore, the lack of leadership and managerial responsibilities that come with authority causes inefficiency and leads to further corruption.

Another stumbling block to Indian economic development is the high illiteracy rate, 33 per cent among men and up to 60 per cent among women.[6] In addition, the agriculture sector, which comprises the largest portion of Indian industry, is also very inefficient. This is a good example of the underdeveloped-nation-style economic pattern where political logic is placed above economic logic. Since the government subsidizes the sector and purchases grain at a high price in the name of agricultural protection, grain prices are higher than international levels, thus burdening the non-agricultural population. This 'subsidy and high-price' policy leads to inefficient agriculture as well as affecting the agricultural population negatively, in the end increasing the national burden.

In a government–business collusion that is typical of underdeveloped countries, traditional conglomerates, including Tata and

Vilas, still dominate the Indian economy. Only recently has the emergence of new conglomerates such as Yulayans, Hinduya and Yubi begun to activate internal competition. Such change was brought about by political reform. The opposition party overpowered the Indian National Congress in all the state governments and accomplished a regime change, thereby securing considerable power in the central government. If global trends and the wave of reform at home are harmonized, India will be able to re-emerge as a new power.

Reshaping the world's power structure and India's role

If India and Bangladesh are included as members, New Asia, as the largest economic bloc, with 2.8 billion people, will have an equal footing with any other economic blocs, such as the NAFTA and the EU. If New Asia maintains an annual average growth rate of over 7 per cent for two decades, it will be able to serve as an engine for development, accounting for two-thirds of the world economy. In this context, the birth of New Asia is the most realistic alternative for the peaceful unity and prosperity of the world. In view of current international trends too, it can be said that the USA incapable of overpowering the EU on its own, became an APEC member in order to ally itself with Asia and to put pressure on the EU through it. As the USA stepped up its influence through measures such as leading the APEC summit talks, the EU suggested the formation of the ASEM to Asia.

Asia, now breaking away from its past isolation, has become dramatically dependent on world economies and has established a triangular structure with the EU and the NAFTA. Asia will be connected to the EU through the ASEM and to the NAFTA through the APEC; and the EU and the NAFTA will maintain a firm co-operation structure through the TAFTA.

If India succeeds in correcting its political system and reforming its economy, its giant potential will expand hugely, causing a chain reaction of development among neighbouring countries. In fact, India, although having enjoyed war-related benefits and being equipped with all the necessary factors for economic development, has never succeeded in development because of its political exclusivity. Fortunately, however, as China achieved high-level economic development through liberalization and economic reforms, reflections on past practices and a sense of crisis are on the rise in India after being stimulated by China. India is therefore becoming closer to Asia with great speed, and trying to re-enact the Asian economic miracle by following Asia's development formula.

Notes

1. Since its independence, India has pushed for the government-led planned economy under the principle of self-sufficiency and self-rehabilitation. Accordingly, India had adhered to a permission policy towards domestic businesses and an entry restriction policy towards foreign businesses. This control-orientated economic system, however, has thrust India into a dilemma of chronic government regulation.
2. The content of deregulation-orientated economic reforms includes the abolishment of the industrial permission system; the liberalization of foreign currency and capital markets; the upward modification of the foreign capital ownership ceiling (51 per cent); and tariff reduction.
3. Foreign investment in labour-intensive industries, targeting domestic markets such as clothes, is not much encouraged because these industries are seen as being able to be fostered with their own technology.
4. India has the greatest number of science and technology personnel in Asia, third only to Japan and China. The number was 119 027 in 1988.
5. As for public enterprises stricken by chronic deficits, the Indian government is pushing for reforms of profit-making and management methods, institutionalized the introduction of professional managers, and is expanding the participation of public-business workers in management.
6. The overall adult illiteracy rate is 49.4 per cent but taking into account differences among states, the rate straddles the 20–80 per cent band.

References

The Economist Intelligence Unit (1997) 'India', *The Economist.*
International Monetary Fund (1997) *Directory of Trade Statistics Yearbook.*
League of Nations (1995) *Statistical Yearbook of the League of Nations.*
Robert Lloyd George (1992) *The East-West Pendulum* (Simon & Schuster).
Mitsubishi Research Institute (1996) *Total Forecasting of Asia.*

11
ASEAN: Catalyst for New Asia

The Association of South-east Asian Nations (ASEAN) was established in August 1967 with five members – Indonesia, Malaysia, The Philippines, Thailand and Singapore. Later, the membership was expanded to seven, with the entry of Brunei and Vietnam, and by the year 2000, it is expected to grow to ten with Laos, Myanmar and Cambodia as new members. ASEAN nations are very different in many ways but at the same time share similarities. They vary culturally, with different ethnic groups, languages and religions, as well as politically and economically, being at different stages of development. Nevertheless, there are similarities in that they share similar positions in diplomacy and security, and pursue similar political and economic goals.

Every ASEAN nation has transformed its economy and industrial structure very quickly from a resources-orientated economy to one focused on manufacturing, and from a labour-intensive structure to a capital- and technology-intensive one. During these processes, all the nations have achieved considerable economic success. However, at the time of writing the region is at the very epicentre of a financial meltdown in South-east Asia, and these countries, including Thailand, are facing their worst economic crisis. The possibility of a moratorium is even being raised. The weakness of the region's economic growth had accumulated in secret before finally being exposed in the current economic blowout. For these ASEAN countries to restart on the road to economic growth, they must implement a full-scale restructuring of existing systems and establish a transparent democratic political structure. But, most important, a

Table 11.1   Economic indicators of four major ASEAN countries, 1995

	The Philippines	Indonesia	Thailand	Malaysia
GDP (US$ billions)	74	203	161	82*
Per capita GDP (US$)	1 083	1 120	2 663	4 042
Economic growth rate (%)	4.8	8.2	8.6	9.5
Consumer price rate of increase (%)	8.1	9.4	5.8	3.4
Exports (US$ billions)	14	52	53	73
Imports (US$ billions)	21	47	61	73
Trade ratio to GDP (%)	47	42.7	70.8	179.6
Foreign reserve (US$ billions) (excluding gold)	6.4	13.7	35.9	23.8
Foreign debt (US$ billions)	42.3	100.2	73.4	27.9

Note: *Estimate.
Source: The Economist Intelligence Unit (1997) *National Sources.*

mental rearmament of the people is desperately needed. The governments of the ASEAN countries must also devise a new formula for development within the larger 'New Asia' framework, based on the increase in interregional trade volume. The concurrent currency depreciation of ASEAN countries has, paradoxically, strengthened the awareness of the need for, and advantages of, interregional trade. A chain of plummeting exchange rates among South-east Asian nations triggered by the downfall of the Thailand baht is an example of how closely interdependent are these nations.

Indonesia

Indonesia is a large tropical island-state comprising some 13 000 islands of various sizes. It is a huge country, with a land area of 2027 000k m^2 and a population of 196 million. However, being an island-state, its land utilization rate is low and a diverse ethnic composition hampers national efficiency. Furthermore, following Suharto's resignation, political instability is further aggravating economic stagnation. Yet, considering the country's rich natural resources and labour power, Indonesia leads other countries in the region in terms of growth potential.

Only about 6000 of the 13 000 Indonesian islands, which have around 400 dormant and extinct volcanoes are inhabited. Over two-thirds of the total population is concentrated on Java, Bali and Sumatra. Java, an island where a large population has lived since ancient times, has the largest population and controls Indonesian politics.

Indonesia became known economically with the start of the spice trade. Indonesia gained commercial importance when Arabian merchants carried spices to Europe in the fourteenth century, and the country was developed as Spain and Portugal cultivated their sea routes. It was around this time that Islam was introduced by Arabian merchants and the religion spread widely. In the late 1990s, 90 per cent of the population are Muslims. Like many other South-east Asian nations, Indonesia also has many Chinese residents. The Chinese people who flowed in at the time of the Mongol invasions have settled in the country and firmly established their roots there.

Indonesia is linguistically very complicated. Although the official language is Javanese, there are about twenty-five major languages in addition to some 250 dialects, making communication between regions difficult. Indonesia had long been under colonial rule. The Netherlands developed Indonesia as a full-scale colony from 1579 and continued its rule, despite interruptions for five years from 1811 by Britain, and by Japan for three years from 1942 to the end of the Second World War.

As a result of President Achmad Sukarno's independence movement, in 1949 Indonesia put an end to this long colonial rule and achieve independence. Sukarno afterwards insisted on a dictatorship and, in order to strengthen his rule, he attempted a government-inspired coup in 1965. However, through a military coup, Thojib Suharto, who was then commander-in-chief of the army, seize political power. Suharto was inaugurated as president in 1966 and held on to power until 1998. Suharto suggested five ruling principles of national foundation based on religion, unification, humanism and social democracy. These principles established authoritarian social and political systems where the welfare of all was placed above individual freedom, based on strengthened traditional patriarchism.

Despite favourable production conditions such as abundant resources and a large workforce, Indonesia has a lower per capita national income than its South-east Asian neighbours. The main reason for this is that Indonesia had been under a politically primitive military dictatorship. During the 1950s, because Indonesia was isolated internationally as a result of Sukarno's military rule, it did not have many trading partners other than Communist countries. Suharto, on taking office in the 1960s, opened Indonesia to the outside world and made strenuous efforts to attract foreign capital for resource development, but to little avail. It was not until the 1990s that Indonesia started to attract attention as a processing export base, utilizing its low-income workforce when wages rose in neighbouring South-east Asian countries such as Thailand.

Despite such poor conditions at home, Indonesia was able to maintain high annual average growth rates – 7.7 per cent during 1971–80; 5.5 per cent during 1981–90; and 8 per cent in 1996. This is probably because it is located in the furnace of development called 'Asia'. However, the substance of growth was not as healthy, as reflected in the high inflation rates of 17.5 per cent in the 1970s; 8.6 per cent in the 1980s; and 6.7 per cent in 1996.

An economic growth pattern such as this is not limited to Indonesia; it can be found in most ASEAN nations. Nevertheless, these countries are continuing their growth through collective inter-action because of Japan's economic strategies. Japan, with a con-tinuing rise in wages and production costs domestically, steadily invested in South-east Asia in order to overcome these at home as well as to pre-empt future markets. When the USA and Europe, Japan's biggest markets, put in place various import restriction devices including a quota system, Japan, in an attempt to circum-vent such devices, made full-scale inroads into South-east Asia.

Japan maintained a highly diversified investment portfolio varying with the investment conditions of each South-east Asian country. Despite its high-risk nature, Indonesia was attractive because of its large domestic market, and Japan's aggressive invest-ments helped to restructure the Indonesian economy. As a conse-quence, the proportion of agriculture in GDP shrank, from 36.8 per cent in 1975 to 17.2 per cent in 1995, while that of manufacturing rose, from 11.1 per cent to 24.3 per cent during the same period. However, primary product processing industries still account for a major segment, with food products at 11.8 per cent, textile products at 12.5 per cent, and wood products at 12.8 per cent. The economic structure is therefore very shaky and the speed of reorganization slow.

This shaky industrial structure is also reflected in exports. In 1995, priority exports of petroleum accounted for 14.2 per cent; gas, 8.8 per cent; wood and plywood, 7.6 per cent; textiles, 6.2 per cent; and rubber, 4.9 per cent. Although the proportion of primary prod-ucts such as petroleum and gas showed considerable decreases, the country's industrial structure still lags behind that of its neighbours.

Exports to Japan, which were 42 per cent in 1989 decreased to 28.8 per cent in 1996 and those to the USA, also for 1996 were 16.5 per cent. However, trade dependency on Asian countries is highest with New Asia[1] accounting for 62.6 per cent[2] of the exports and 55.4 per cent[3] of the imports. Hence, Indonesia is highly depend-ent on other Asian countries.

Insufficient investment in education categorizes Indonesia as a country with the least number of engineers and scientists in spite of its huge population. There are a mere ten science and technology personnel per 1000 population, recording the lowest among ASEAN members. The number of high-quality personnel for research and development is only 1.7 to 1000. Indonesia's middle school attendance rate is 45 per cent, the lowest among all ASEAN members except Vietnam. Six economic development plans achieved very little apart from slight development in infrastructure and agriculture. This is because of the absence of high-quality human resources. The Indonesian government should therefore make investment in education its top priority.

A vast land area comprising a large number of islands and islets creates a high demand for aircraft as a mode of transportation to connect the regions. Accordingly, Science and Technology Minister B. J. Babibie suggested a 'Hi-Tech Industry Development Plan' and established a state-owned aircraft manufacturing corporation called Industri Pesawat Terbang Nusantara (IPTN) in 1976. Since its establishment, IPTN has imported technology for aircraft design, component manufacture and assembly techniques and related personnel to produce medium-size aircraft and helicopters, with a huge investment of over US$20 billion. However, the project is under criticism for being fundamentally shaky as domestic demand is too small in relation to the amount invested and Indonesia's technological base is too unstable to support a hi-tech aviation industry.

In addition, Indonesia is attempting to manufacture automobiles of its own after being inspired by the success of the 'Proton', a Malaysian-made car. But investments such as these, without considering the level of domestic technology, are reducing the possibility of success. Import-substitution projects carried out under government protection will end up burdening consumers with high production costs. Furthermore, the goals of such large-scale investments are merely to serve the propaganda purposes of the omnipotent government and not based on any sound business decisions.[5]

It will be rather difficult for Indonesia, a latecomer, to reach the levels of other countries if it follows their economic development procedures step by step. Indonesia is therefore attempting to bypass such procedures and move directly into hi-tech industries. However, manufacturing that requires massive capital and technological capacity will not accommodate this. Asian NICs have accomplished high growth in such a short period of time that on the surface, it may seem that they have transformed their backward industrial structures into advanced ones overnight by importing foreign technology. But, these countries have not skipped general economic development stages. Condensed growth, where each stage is completed in a very short period of time, made it appear so.

Therefore, it would be better for Indonesia to push forward with its development as a way to solidify its economic base within the larger framework of the New Asian economic bloc. All ASEAN members including Indonesia are rich in human resources[6] and they are relatively cheap despite recent wage rises. Although such factors are still attractive to foreign businesses, many foreign investors conclude that the quality of labour is so low that wages are not cheap in relation to productivity. Most urgent for Indonesia, therefore, is to improve the educational level of the people as soon as possible.

Most important, the future of Indonesia hinges on how the political chaos is managed and whether the country is able to establish a new political framework in the post-Suharto years. Considerable pain is expected in the course of the country's democratic development. However, Indonesia's economic potential is greater than those of other South-east Asian countries and hence, in the long run, it is highly possible that the country will emerge as a regional power.

Thailand

Thailand, the only country in East Asia without colonial experience, has exerted great influence as a regional power throughout its history. Thailand was able to overcome invasions by the Western colonial forces, and threats from neighbouring superpowers, partly because of its geopolitical advantages of being protected as a military buffer zone by neighbours. However, it is mainly because of its efficient politics.

The strong ruling power of the Chakri dynasty founded in 1782 prevented the West from colonizing Thailand. Located in the middle of Indochina peninsula, Thailand has fertile plains around the Chaopraya river that occupy most of the land. With a land area of 510 000 km^2, a population of 58 million, GDP of US$183.6 billion, and per capita GDP of US$2994, Thailand has economic power comparable to that of South Korea, when reassessed by purchasing power valuation.

The majority of the population of Thailand are Thai, who migrated from Funan province of China long ago. Thailand has a relatively short history compared to other Asian countries. The Thai-founded

Sukothai dynasty (1238–1350) was the first Thai state and this was followed by the Ayuttaya (1448–1767) and the Chakri (1782–). Rama V (1853–1910), who ascended the throne in 1868, accepted Western culture and established the bureaucratic system, thus modernizing the country. As a result, Thailand, unlike the rest of the Indochinese countries, was not occupied by Japan. Thailand, however, assisted Japan in its war efforts and provided an advance base for Japan in capturing Malaysia.

A coup in 1932 paved the way for a full-scale intervention of the military in politics, and the military regime still holds power. Phibun, in particular, established the political framework of modern Thailand with his dictatorship during 1948–57 and changed the then official name of the country from Siam to Thailand.

Thailand has maintained high growth since the 1970s, recording an average GDP growth rate of 8 per cent. Inflation was 10 per cent in the 1970s; 4.4 per cent in the 1980s; and 5.8 per cent in 1996, thus maintaining a very stable level for a developing country. But it was robust savings and investment that have brought success to Thailand. The savings ratio went up from 22.2 per cent in the 1970s to 35 per cent in the 1980s. Domestic investment also increased steadily, from 25.3 per cent to 34.3 per cent in 1994. Continued high growth requires high savings and investment ratios of above 30 per cent, and Thailand is meeting this requirement.

The interest rate burden of total exports fell from 14.5 per cent in the 1970s to a stabilized level of 11 per cent in 1994. Nevertheless, bubbles such as sudden wage rises, political unrest, ostentatious consumption trends, lax management, and real estate speculation prevented Thailand from coping with the deteriorating international economic situation. The loss of export competitiveness increased the current account deficit level to over US\$1 million after 1995, and to an alarming US\$1.47 million in 1996. Furthermore, in 1997, the Thailand baht depreciated by more than 25 per cent having a ripple effect on the rest of the world. Because of low-priced Chinese-made products that are flooding the international markets, Thailand's export competitiveness is weakening rapidly.

In Thailand's economic structure, the proportion of the agricultural sector has fallen by more than half from 24.8 per cent in 1975 to 10.9 per cent in 1995, and that of the manufacturing sector has increased, from 19.9 per cent to 30.2 per cent during the same period.

In the export structure as well, food and food products, which are primary processed exports, showed a visible decrease from 83.6 per cent in 1989 to 21.5 per cent in 1993, while machinery surged from 17.8 per cent to 30 per cent during the same period. These figures reflect a dramatic industrial restructuring effort by the Thai government. In 1995, computers and related components, and textiles accounted for large proportions of the total, with 10 per cent and 10.2 per cent respectively. Among its trading partners, the proportion of the USA and the EU fell to 17.9 per cent and 16 per cent in 1996, respectively, while that of ASEAN members soared from 11.5 per cent in 1989 to 19.3 per cent in 1996. Thus, the main focus of Thailand's trade is gradually transferring to its Asian neighbours.

Around 36 per cent of foreign investment in Thailand is made by Hong Kong, Taiwan and Singapore. What deserves attention here is that the dynamics of South-east Asian economies stem basically from intraregional trade. Japan, the largest investor, accounts for 40–60 per cent of the total foreign investment in Thailand. Japan prefers Thailand as an overseas production base because Thailand is a Buddhist nation.

The development of East Asia stems from a policy of industrialization. The main capital providers are Japan and the NICs, and a considerable amount of exports are taking place within the region. All this proves that the environment for East Asian economic integration is almost ready. Despite its considerable degree of industrialization, Thailand had a 60 per cent agricultural population in 1995. Therefore if, during the industrialization process, the unemployed population is diverted to the manufacturing sector, the economic growth of Thailand will pick up speed.

Thailand is expected to suffer considerable discomfort in the course of democratization in the foreseeable future. Thailand's military dictatorship, which began in 1938, is quite different from those in other countries. First of all, the royal family function as a mediator between the people and the regime based on the absolute trust of the people, thereby decreasing the possibility of extreme confrontations. Second, although there is a military regime, power has been dispersed to some extent because of incessant coups. These factors provide Thailand with some degree of flexibility to overcome future changes. Thailand's potential for economic development is larger than that of its Asian neighbours.

Malaysia

With a land area covering 330 000 km², Malaysia is a disproportionately large country for a population of 21.2 million This is mainly because of the northern region, where Borneo, an island, is larger than the mainland. The aggressive policies by the Mahathir administration to attract foreign investment established the export-led high growth system, resulting in the rapid growth of the country. At the time of writing, Malaysia's GDP is US$99.2 billion, with per capital GNP US$4697, giving the country an economic scale half that of Thailand.

Malaysia welcomed large numbers of foreigners for resource development during British rule. As a consequence, the population structure became complicated, making national integration difficult.[7] Nevertheless, nationwide enthusiasm for economic development will unite the people as long as economic development continues and the ethnic diversity can, in turn, become a point of strength. The developmental process of East Asian economies can be summarized as follows. The experiences of Japan, the pacesetter of economic development in the region, spread to South Korea and Taiwan, and later to South-east Asia. Malaysia, ever since Mahathir bin Muhammad urged his countrymen to 'Look East', has accomplished rapid economic development by emulating Japan and South Korea.

Originally, Malaysia was not a unified nation but a country composed of many states ruled by sultans. Since there were many countries involved when Portugal captured Malacca, Portugal traded separately with each of them. After the Dutch invasion in 1641, however, Malacca lost its position as a trading centre. Later, in 1786, Great Britain used Penang as a transit base for exporting opium to China in order to correct the trade imbalance.

After occupying Malacca in 1795 and Singapore in 1919, Britain united Penang, Malacca and Singapore in 1826 into a colony called the 'Straits Settlement'. The British East India Company first, took control of the Settlements, but in 1876 Malaysia came under the direct rule of the British Colonial Administration.

However, the strong British power was neutralized by Japan and this led to the birth of the Malaysian Federation in 1948. Indonesia, threatened by the formation of a strong federation in its vicinity, waged a guerrilla war, and as a result Malaysia seceded from the Malaysian Federation in 1965 to become an independent state. The reasons are as follows: first, if the three million Chinese living in Singapore united, the number of Chinese would almost equal that of Malays, thus depriving them of political initiative. Second, the Philippines and Indonesia opposed the formation of a strong federation.

Although comprising a majority of 59 per cent of the population, Malays are economically poor, while the Chinese, with 31 per cent of the population, have control of the economy. Because of this, a system was established where Malays were superior in politics, and the Chinese in the economy. Nevertheless, hostilities between the two continued to grow stronger before finally erupting in riots in 1969. The government, in order to resolve the situation, stepped up its intervention and enabled Malays to occupy up to 30 per cent of all capital by 1997. The basis of the policy was to distribute the products of the expanded economy to natives, giving 30 per cent ownership to them. The government thought that for inter-ethnic peace, at least about 30 per cent of wealth should be given to the natives, who comprise 60 per cent of the population.

The economic policies of Prime Minister Mahathir has changed Malaysia dramatically since 1981. The emphasis of his policies was placed on structural changes of the economy. Accordingly, the proportion of agriculture shrank from 27.7 per cent in 1975 to 12.8 per cent in 1996, while that of manufacturing soared from 16.4 per cent to 34.3 per cent making Malaysia the most industrialized nation in South-east Asia. Because of such swift industrial reorganization centring on manufacturing[8] those who worked in manufacturing increased from 15.9 per cent in 1985 to 25.9 per cent in 1995. In particular, the proportion in the electric, electronics, and textile industries rose from 35.6 per cent in 1985 to 51.6 per cent in 1995.[9]

The high average GDP growth of 7.8 per cent in the 1970's was consistently maintained through 1997 while inflation was 2.7 per cent in 1997, down from 6 per cent in 1970. The savings ratio went up from 29.1 per cent in the 1970's to 40 per cent in 1994, laying the foundations for continued high growth.

Also, the financial costs of exports shrank from 4.2 per cent in 1970 to 5 per cent in 1994, thus proving sound financial management. What deserves attention here is the 78 per cent share of manufacturing in the export structure. This robust economic development of

Malaysia stemmed from its aggressive foreign capital inducement policy.[10] In other words, the government, in order to attract hi-tech and capital-intensive manufacturing industries, provided foreign investors with various types of incentive, including tax exemption for the first five years, tax reduction for development and training programmes, and abolition of tax on computer and software sales. Recently, however, Malaysia has been struggling with a chronic current account deficit incurred by remittance of earnings, a side-effect of foreign investment inducement. This is because the two million foreign workers who comprise 20 per cent of the total work force are sending US$1.2 billion back to their respective countries every year. To correct such situation, the Malaysian government is attempting to reorganize the industrial structure from labour-intensive to technology-intensive.

Among the chief exporting partners of Malaysia, Singapore accounts for 20.5 per cent; Japan, 13.4 per cent; the five ASEAN members, 7.6 per cent; and NICs, 10.4 per cent of total exports, reflecting the high dependency on intra-Asia trade. Countries with the highest proportions are Taiwan, Japan and Singapore. Taiwan and Singapore comprise 60 per cent of total investment, proving that capital is also being provided within the Asian region.

Among the US$13.6 billion manufacturing investment in 1996, US$6.77 billion (or 49.8 per cent) came from foreign capital. Exports of goods are also internally dependent. Therefore Indonesia, Thailand and Malaysia all have much higher intraregional economic dependency compared to 1957, when Europe began integration according to the Rome Treaty, casting a favourable light on the future of the New Asian economic integration.

Mahathir recently suggested the formation of the East Asian Economic Group (EAEG) to encourage ASEAN-centred economic integration and the construction of a strong Asia. In line with this, he has since 1996 been pushing for the nurturing of high-quality personnel and a reduction in foreign capital dependence. In most cases, economic development plus powerful leadership brings about efficiency in initial stages, but once it passes a certain point, unexpected side-effects surface. This is because, as an economy reaches a certain level of development, demands for democratization, more spare time, and fewer working hours erupt, thereby weakening the development energy and slowing development.

The Philippines

As a former colony of both Spain and the USA, the Philippines was exposed to Western culture from an early date, and until the 1950s was the most advanced nation in South-east Asia. However, the long-term dictatorship by President Ferdinand Marcos threw the country into political unrest, unequal distribution of wealth and social turmoil, which led to economic devastation. In the late 1990s, per capital GDP is a mere US$1197, and GDP is only US$83.5 billion. Since Marcos stepped down, however, political stability has been regained and the people are enthusiastic about economic development, which makes the country's long-term prospects very positive.

The Philippines is a relatively big country, comprising some 1700 islands, and extend 1107 km east and west and 1851 km north and south (a total land area of 300 000 km²). Most islands, however, have such small coastal plains that the population is only about 70 million. Because of frequent volcanic eruptions and earthquakes, only about 800 islands are inhabited, and most of the population is concentrated in Luzon and Mindanao, the two biggest islands which combined have 66 per cent of the land.

The Philippines was first settled by the Negritos, who migrated from the Asian continent some 15 000 years ago, and some are still living in the mountain highlands of Luzon as a minority group. While Malays are Indonesian and Malaysian origin comprise the largest majority of the population, a considerable number of Chinese also flowed in during migration from Fujian around the tenth century AD. Relatively large numbers of people have also migrated from Spain since the sixteenth century. There has been long period of ethnic mixing among these three groups, resulting in the present-day Filipinos.

The aboriginal inhabitants of the Philippines are split into 126 tribes linguistically. However, most of the languages are similar to Malay, and while the population is divided because of geographic separation as a result of being an island-state, ethnically they share common roots. The official language is Tagalog, and English is the most common language used. An absolute majority of 83 per cent are Catholic, but with 5 per cent Islam and 9 per cent Protestant, the religious structure is complicated.

Since the country was discovered by Ferdinand Magellan in 1521, it has been colonized by Spain and it served as Spanish East Asian base from 1580. The settlement of the Spanish American War in 1898 required Spain to cede the Philippines to the USA and the country then became an East Asian base for the USA. The reason the USA recognized Japanese colonial rule in Korea was to obtain Japan's reciprocal recognition of the US colonization of the Philippines. The Philippines was occupied by Japan in 1941 and reclaimed by the USA in February 1945. However, because the country was of no practical interest, the USA allowed its independence.

The Philippines once had great leaders such as Ramon Magsaysay, but after Marcos was elected President in 1965, placing the country under a long dictatorship, the society became extremely corrupt and the concentration of wealth intensified. Marcos, Benigno-Simeon Aquino, Jr. and even Fidel Valdez Ramos, the present ruler, were all landed gentry who own most of the country's land and wealth. This is why most of the people cannot escape absolute poverty and economic development is not gaining speed.

The economic growth rate fell from 6 per cent in the 1970s to 1 per cent in the 1980s. Despite the election of Aquino as president in 1986, several coups occurred and, because of administrative incapacity caused by the long dictatorship, normal state management was difficult. In the midst of such confusion, however the Philippines managed to record a 5.5 per cent growth in 1996. Nevertheless, at the time of writing, the degree of economic recovery remains insignificant.

Inflation remains relatively high, at 14.8 per cent in the 1970s; 13.3 per cent in the 1980s; and 8.4 per cent in 1996. The savings ratio fell from 26.5 per cent in the 1970s to 19.8 per cent in 1996, and domestic investment recorded 27.8 per cent in the 1970s and 24.8 per cent in 1996, relatively low figures compared to neighbouring countries. The financial costs of exports rose from 13.5 per cent in the 1970s to 24.5 per cent in 1994.

In terms of the country's industrial structure, the agricultural sector, which comprised 24.7 per cent in 1975, took a similar share of 21.4 per cent in 1996, proving that the Philippines is still highly dependent on agriculture. The proportion of manufacturing, however, went down, from 26 per cent in 1975 to 22.6 per cent in 1996, indicating that the primitive economic structure had not been improved. Within manufacturing, foodstuffs, textiles and wood comprise a major part. Although some semiconductors and electrical products are processed and exported, the amount is insufficient to be an economic contribution.[11] The reasons for this are economic instability and the absence of investment incentives that discourage foreign capital. Although it recovered slightly in the 1990s, towards the millennium foreign investment still remains minimal.

As chief trading partners of the Philippines, the USA accounts for 33.9 per cent and the EU 15.9 per cent of total trade, reflecting the country's continuing high dependency on the West, which proves that the Philippines has not yet fully entered the mainstream of East Asia's economic development.

The Philippines government, in addition to MEPE (Mactan Export Processing Zone), is planning to designate Subic Bay, which was handed over by the USA at the end of 1992, as an economic special zone and free port. The government is making efforts to develop the region for a variety of purposes, including ship repair and maintenance service, cargo transit, tourism and manufacturing, by utilizing the facilities and infrastructure of the former US Pacific Fleet headquarters. The Philippines government provides unique tax benefits to regional businesses. In return for 5 per cent of their income, the government exempts these businesses from all national and local taxes.

Conclusions on the four major South-east Asian nations

This review of the four major South-east Asian nations leads us to several conclusions. First, Asian economies laid the foundations for development individually, although Japan had taken the lead. To overcome US or European regulations, Japan began processing exports by investing in neighbouring Taiwan and South Korea. However, as the economic development of these two countries raised income levels, the attraction of low wages disappeared. In the case of South Korea, in particular, anti-Japanese sentiment intensified and the country was no longer attracted Japan investment. Furthermore, with industrial restructuring, South Korea emerged as a competitor, prompting Japan to keep it in check. Japan withdrew from South Korea and made inroads into Malaysia and Thailand. As the wages in those countries also rose, Japan moved again, to the Philippines and Indonesia, and finally to Vietnam and

Myanmar. Therefore, the chain of economic developments in the Asian region has been the unexpected result of Japan's moving its production bases around to maximize its own interests.

These Asian countries, however, are now suffering from the collapse of the bubble economy, similar to Japan's experience in the past. Capital inflow is being funnelled into real estate speculation instead of infrastructure construction and production, resulting in a chain of real estate price rises and the overconsumption that follows. This trend poses a serious threat to the region's economic growth, as the substance of growth is becoming increasingly unhealthy.

Other South-east Asian nations

Cambodia, Vietnam, Myanmar and Laos are the least developed countries in the world. Political factors were the main cause of the delayed economic development in these countries despite relatively favourable natural conditions and abundant resources. All these countries are following the typical pattern of 'exploitation by Western colonial powers → independence → civil wars caused by ideological conflicts → socialist government established → devastated economy'. These Asian latecomers on the path to economic development, can still have a bright future if they avoid their predecessors' mistakes and devise new development formulas.

Naturally, in order to raise their depressed economies up to an acceptable level, these countries will need to emulate certain aspects of their predecessors' development models. However, by utilizing their mild natural surroundings, outstanding scenery and unique cultures, these countries could foster high-income crop-growing, or tourism, as their priority industries. In the twenty-first century, as international specialization is pursued more aggressively, the four Asian latecomers will be able to play important roles within the framework of 'New Asia'.

Cambodia

The Mons and the Khmers had migrated from the north to the southeast before the time of Christ, far earlier than their neighbours, the Vietnamese, the Lao, and the Thai. The early Cambodian dynasties imitated Indian culture in virtually all areas, including their alphabet, religion, architecture and social class systems. During the prosperous Angkor era of the Khmer kingdom, Cambodia was home to a powerful and highly advanced Buddhist and Hindu civilization. Nevertheless, the dynasty declined because of invasions by Siam (Thailand), and Vietnam and Cambodia suffered through incessant invasions. After being invaded by France when the Western colonial forces entered Indochina and by Japan during the Second World War, Cambodia finally attained independence in 1953.

In 1970, while King Sihanouk was abroad, the Lon Nol regime was established through a coup led by the right-wing military. The regime changed the name of the country to the Khmer Republic and adopted pro-US and pro-Western policies. In 1975, after ousting Sihanouk, a democratic Cambodian government was founded, with Kiu Sampan as the head of state and Pol Pot as the prime minister. The pro-chinese socialist reform policies of the government, however, led to conflicts with pro-Soviet Vietnam. Finally in January 1979, the Vietnam-backed Heng Samrin toppled the Pol Pot regime and established the People's Republic of Cambodia with a pro-Vietnamese propensity.

For thirteen exhausting years after this, the country was engulfed in violent domestic conflicts, which devastated the production bases of Cambodia. To make matters worse, allies, including the USSR and Vietnam, stopped economic and military aid, thus hurling the country into far worse ruins. Since 1989, however, Cambodia has steadfastly pushed for economic reform based on price decontrol, recognition of private ownership, the privatization of state-owned enterprises, and the introduction of a foreign investment law. With the general election held under United Nations (UN) supervision in May 1993, the nation's credit standing improved dramatically. All this led to increases in foreign investments and economic aid. Accordingly, GDP surged from US$2 billion in 1993 to US$3.1 billion in 1996, and per capita income also went up to US$290.

Recent economic development in Cambodia, however, has been led by construction and service-related industries composed mainly of accommodation and restaurant businesses, a stark contrast to its neighbouring countries that are maintaining high growth based on manufacturing. Industries such as services and construction showed high growth with increased aid from international organizations including the UN. But manufacturing is showing extremely low growth because of primitive production facilities and inferior

Table 11.2   Cambodia's major economic indicators

	1993	1996
Population (millions)	9.7	10.7
Current GDP (US$ billions)	2.0	3.1
Consumer price increasing rate (%)	114.3	9.0
Exports (US$ billions)	0.28	0.6
Imports (US$ billions)	0.47	1.1
Foreign reserves (US$ billions) (exluding gold)	0.024	0.3
Foreign debt (US$ billions)	0.38	2.1
Economic growth rate (%)	4.1	6.5

Source: The Economist Intelligence Unit (1999) 'Cambodia', *The Economist.*

productivity by state-owned businesses, continuing political unrest, and widespread smuggling along the borders.

As a consequence in 1996, the proportion of services and agriculture in GDP was 37.4 per cent and 42.7 per cent respectively, while manufacturing including construction was a mere 19.9 per cent. Therefore, despite the recovery in economic growth, Cambodia has a weak foundation for self-sustained development.

Among exports, agricultural products such as rubber, wood, corn and soya beans account for the largest portion.[12] Among imports, petroleum products, cement and machinery comprise the largest. Since the 1990s, imports of consumption goods, such as garments, textiles and construction materials, have been increasing rapidly.[13] Among chief trading partners, since the government accelerated economic liberalization in the 1990s. New Asia accounted for 56 per cent of total exports and 90.3 per cent of total imports, showing that Cambodia's trade is concentrated in Asia.

Cambodia, which put an end to long domestic strife and returned to the market system, is making strenuous efforts to formulate policies to activate the economy, including economic stabilization and restructuring; infrastructure expansion; the expansion of private ownership; and the development of rural areas. Nevertheless, the country is still deep in a quagmire of structural weakness such as political instability, a corrupt bureaucracy, financial deficits, capital and technological incapacity, agriculture-dependent industrial structure, and weak key industries. These factors overshadow the future of the Cambodian economy.

However, if Asian economic leaders, including Japan, accelerate the speed of technology transfer and investment following Cambodia's entry into ASEAN, the country can grow into another NIC. The Cambodian government should develop aggressive incentives for foreign capital inducement and, more important, should not repeat the mistakes of current ASEAN members.

Vietnam

Located in the eastern part of the Indochina peninsula, Vietnam shares borders with China to the north and with Laos and Cambodia to the west. Two major rivers flow east and west in Vietnam – the Red river in the north and the Mekong river in the south. Originating in Tibet and extending 4180 km, the Mekong ends in the fertile Mekong delta. Vietnam, with a population of 73 million, is made up of various ethnic groups, but the Vietnamese themselves comprise 88 per cent of the total. The Vietnamese initially founded a unified state called Nam Viet (meaning South Viet). However, enduring a 1000-year-long Chinese rule, three Mongol invasions, and the establishment of the Chinese-style bureaucratic government with the second invasion of China, Vietnam has been greatly influenced by China, both politically and culturally.

In 1802, after being unified by General Nguyen Anh, Vietnam actively engaged in trade with Thailand, using European missionaries as middlemen. Since the missionaries intervened in politics, however, King Ming Mang persecuted them, prompting the French to colonize Vietnam. Resisting the French rule, Communists and nationalists under the lead of Ho Chi Minh declared independence in 1945. After victory in the first Indochinese war with France, Vietnam was divided, into the Soviet-supported North and the US-supported South, at latitude 17° North according to the Geneva Agreement in 1954. In the Vietnam War with the USA in 1964 Vietnam emerged victorious, and in conflicts triggered by discrimination against Chinese residents, Vietnam stood up to the powerful China. In both cases, Vietnam prevailed over superpowers far more powerful than itself and emerged as a military leader in Indochina. Nevertheless, the corrupted administration, inefficient bureaucracy, and the imbalance of the local economies led to the failure of economic revival and the deterioration of international relations, ultimately isolating the country.

Table 11.3   Vietnam's major economic indicators

	1993	1996*
Population (millions)	69.3	78.5
Current GDP (US$ billions)	9.9	27.0
Consumer price increasing rate (%)	37.8	3.1
Exports (US$ billions)	2.6	8.9
Imports (US$ billions)	2.5	11.2
Foreign reserves (US$ billions) (excluding gold)	1.2	2.2
Foreign debt (US$ billions)	4.1	9.9
Economic growth rate (%)	8.7	8.8

Note: *Estimate
Source: The Economist Intelligence Unit (1999) 'Vietnam', *The Economist.*

In spite of favourable factors such as fertile soil, a mild climate that enables multiple cropping, and abundant natural resources, Vietnam remains in poverty because of an infrastructure devastated by economic sanctions, war, and a backward industrial structure. Even agriculture, Vietnam's chief industry, 95 per cent of which is done by mass production, has very low productivity, and, worse, its trade is monopolized by state-owned businesses.[14] Vietnamese, the official language, is written in the Roman alphabet, a unique case in East Asia, which to a large extent bears the influence of French colonial rule.

Vietnam's continuing socialist economic system has resulted in widespread productivity decreases, a loss of willingness to work, and shortages of daily necessities. Until the mid-1980's when the Doi Moi[15] policy designed to open domestic market and introduce a market economy system was promoted, Vietnam was an economically backward country. The inefficient socialist economic system resulted in extremely low productivity, loss of motivation to work, and a serious lack of daily necessities. The inflation rate approached an alarming 700 per cent and the amount gained from exports hovered at half of the foreign currency amount spent on imports. This policy targeted market opening and the introduction of a market economy system. In the initial stages of the reform, Vietnam experienced difficulties because of the termination of Soviet aid, an insufficient supply of goods, unemployment increases, and extreme inflation. Nevertheless, Vietnam has been recording high growth of 8–9 per cent per year during the 1990s. As a result, per capita GDP soared from US$150 in 1986 to US$270 in 1995, and trade volume also increased, from US$4 billion in the early stages of the reform to US$19.0 billion in 1997.[16] Foreign trade volume recorded a remarkable annual average growth rate of 20 per cent during 1991–5. Among chief exporting partners, Japan accounts for 26.4 per cent; the EU, 24.3 per cent; and New Asia, 55.1 per cent.

Several factors, including the normalization of diplomatic ties with the USA and membership in ASEAN, enabled the Vietnamese government successfully to attract foreign capital. As major countries such as Japan and the USA intensified investment, the amount of foreign investment in Vietnam for the single year 1995 reached US$7.6 billion, 70 per cent of the total investments made during the previous seven years. Foreign-invested businesses accounted for 8.3 per cent of total exports and 20 per cent of the manufacturing exports in 1994.

As such, foreign capital which was mainly concentrated in the manufacturing sector, played a major part in Vietnam's economic development. Following the recent economic depression of Asian countries, US$1.65 billion of foreign capital was newly invested in the country on 181 different occasions between January and September 1998.[17]

Myanmar

Myanmar, known as Burma before 1989, is a small country with a relatively small population of 43 million compared to its large land size of 678 528 km². The Burmese, who had migrated from Tibet around the ninth century, constitute the majority. In the eleventh century, with the founding of the Pagan dynasty, Myanmar became a unified kingdom. Later in the thirteenth century, however, the country was divided into many ethnic groups following the Mongol invasion. Burma once again flourished with the establishment of the Toungoo dynasty in the mid-sixteenth century, but it came under British rule with the Western occupation that had begun in the seventeenth century.

Great Britain promoted large-scale rice farming in the Sittang Delta to utilize it as a food provision base for India, and Chinese and Indians seized control of the small- and medium-sized commerce and distribution networks of the country. Such foreign incursions ignited nationalism and encouraged to national unity, but stripped the country economically and pushed it toward impoverishment. In 1948, Burma attained independence and the federal government was established. The government expelled foreign capital and nationalized all remaining capital, but because of the ensuing social disorder and inefficiency of the socialist economic system, the move resulted in an weakened economy. The national energy that accumulated as a response to incessant foreign incursions erupted in the form of the indiscriminate exclusion of anything foreign.

By 1976, the economy had recovered to some extent, with an economic development policy based on foreign capital inducement. However, the country at one time faced a serious crisis stemming from accumulated foreign debts and decreased rice production. After recording a high growth rate of 9.7 per cent in 1992, Myanmar's continues to show favourable signs and the growth rate is expected to reach 5.8 per cent in 1996. Accordingly, GDP is expected to increase, from US$40.9 billion in 1992 to US$125.8 billion in 1996, and per capita GDP from US$93.6 billion to US$267.7 billion during the same period. The consumer price rate, however, increased to a high 20–30 per cent in the 1990s because of financial deficits and increased issuance of currency as well as the commodities shortages that followed. However, as a result of the government's price stabilization efforts, the rate is expected to record a relatively low 16.3 per cent in 1996.

Myanmar is primarily an agricultural country, with agriculture comprising 53.4 per cent of GDP, and manufacturing a mere 7.3 per

Table 11.4   Myanmar's major economic indicators

	1992	1996
Population (millions)	43.7	45.6
Current GDP (US$ billions)	40.9	125.8
Consumer price rate of increase (%)	21.9	16.3
Exports (US$ billions)	0.59	0.9
Imports (US$ billions)	1.01	1.6
Foreign reserves (US$ billions) (excluding gold)	0.28	0.23
Foreign debt (US$ billions)	5.36	5.77
Economic growth rate (%)	9.7	5.8

Source: The Economist Intelligence Unit (1997) 'Myanmar', *The Economist.*

cent. Under the socialist economic system, the government long monopolized the trade sector. With permission for private participation in the sector, however, imports and exports are increasing rapidly.

Among exports, agricultural products, including beans and rice, and forest products such as rubber comprise about two-thirds of the total amount. Chief trading partners are Singapore, Japan, China and India. Of export transactions, 65.1 per cent, and imports, 86.6 per cent are with New Asian nations, which indicates that Myanmar maintains very close economic relations with New Asian members, as with other South-east Asian countries. The reform policy of Myanmar is dramatically increasing foreign direct investment. The amount reached US$3084 million by the end of 1995. Major investors are Britain, Singapore, France and Thailand.

Though once designated by the UN as the world's poorest country, and despite the fact that the USA is restricting new investment and trade because of the government's crackdown on democratization movements, Myanmar faces a new phase of economic development after its official entry into ASEAN in May 1997. Foreign capital investment will become a crucial variable to the success of the economy, therefore, a more open and democratized economic environment is in order.

Laos

Laos is an inland state surrounded by China, Vietnam, Thailand and Myanmar. Despite the mild climate and fertile soil, Laos is one of the poorest countries in the world, with a per capita national income of only US$355. The climate of Laos is basically tropical but wide variations in temperature occur in different areas because of varying degrees of elevation. It is an agricultural country whose main product is rice from the fertile farms around the Mekong river.

The first group of settlers were the people called the Kha who lived in Funan province of China from before the fifth century AD. They came under the domination of the Chenla kingdom, the early Khmer kingdom. Later, the Lao tribe, a branch of the Thai clan, flowed in from South China and constituted a majority. At the time of writing they make up half of the total population. The geographical features of Laos have created a complex population structure. Besides the Lao, the Laotian population consists of the

Lao Theung, who are of Indonesian origin; the Meo and Yao of Sino-Tibetan origin; and small minority groups of Chinese and Vietnamese.

Physically surrounded by superpowers, Laos has long suffered from incessant invasions. It shares the experience of European colonial rule with the rest of its Indochinese neighbours. In 1893 a French expedition captured most of the major cities of Laos and forced the then Siam (Thailand) to recognize the Laotian territories east of the Mekong river as a French colony. Although France colonized Laos in 1904, because the region was still under the control of Siam, it ruled indirectly through the king of Louangphrabang in the west of Laos on the Mekong river.

In 1949, Laos attained independence from the French Union. Accordingly, many leaders of ethnic independence movement, who had fled to other countries at the time of the second French invasion, returned home. However, the followers of Prince Souphanouvong, did not agree with their opinions and went on to form an alliance with the pro-Communist Vietnamese independence coalition called the 'Vietminh', which was engaged in an war of independence with France in Vietnam at that time. The followers, who were called the 'Pathet Lao', joined forces with the Vietminh and invaded Laos in 1953.

With the end of the Indochinese war in 1954, Laos gained independence as a buffer country between Vietnam and Thailand. The Pathet Lao defeated the government troops and took the helm of the country in 1975. Afterwards, Laos maintained a close relationship with Vietnam and became a member of the Indochina alliance.

In 1986, Laos launched a policy called 'Pean pang mai', meaning 'new thought', to convert the controlled economy to a market system, and achieved a high growth of 6–8 per cent annually. Nevertheless, the policy failed to bring about real success because of the suspension of Soviet aid, labour shortages, and failed attempts to encourage foreign investments. A poor crop yield, in particular, raised prices that had previously been relatively stable to an unstable double-digit level. In the GDP breakdown in 1996, agriculture/forestry was the highest, with 54.3 per cent. Manufacturing, including construction, was a mere 18.8 per cent, and services only 24.5 per cent.

Table 11.5   Laos's major economic indicators

	1992	1995	1996
Population (millions)	4.47	4.87	n/a
Current GDP (US$ billions)	1.2	1.7	1.9
Consumer prices rate of increase (%)	9.9	19.6	13.1
Exports (US$ billions)	0.13	0.35	0.32
Imports (US$ billions)	0.23	0.54	0.64
Foreign reserves (US$ billions) (excluding gold)	0.04	0.09	0.17
Foreign debt (US$ billions)	1.9	2.2	2.3
Economic growth rate (%)	7.1	7.0	6.8

Source: The Economist Intelligence Unit (1997) ' Laos', *The Economist.*

The largest investor is Thailand, comprising 42.3 per cent of the total investments, amounting to US$1.9 billion, while the USA invested US$1.5 billion. These investments are mainly concentrated on resources development. Such foreign investment boosted exports and imports to US$323 million and US$690 million, respectively, in 1996. Among the chief exporting partners, Vietnam accounted for 39 per cent, ranking first, followed by Thailand with 19.6 per cent. With respect to major importing partners, Thailand ranked first with 63.9 per cent, followed by Japan with 6.3 per cent, Vietnam with 4.8 per cent, and China with 3.8 per cent.

Closing comments

It was Japan's incredible economic growth that revealed the potential of Asian economies. Japan's success gave confidence and an aim to Asian countries. It was also Japan that ignited the region's economic development. Although Japan's advance into Asia was propelled by self-interest to secure markets and utilize low-wage labour, it is nevertheless true that Japan consequently contributed positively to Asian economic development.

Japan had long been exploring the possibility of turning East Asia into its domestic market. A full-scale market advance began in earnest when the country could no longer turn a profit with only domestic production. Even the introduction of marginal technology that was already outdated in Japan was able to improve productivity in other Asian nations. Technology and capital that escaped from

Japan for survival spread to its East Asian neighbours in stages. The chain of technological innovation that followed was the fuse that ignited East Asian economic development.

East Asia has a huge population as well as providing potential markets. Furthermore, the agricultural population has largely shifted to manufacturing, thus boosting productivity. With strengthened purchasing power arising from income increases, the markets of the technology-providing nations were also broadened. Front-runners push more aggressively for technology introduction and development in order not to fall behind their competitors. Therefore, when a country reaches a higher level of development, it affects other nations, thereby creating a chain of expansive reproduction.

The foundations of the manufacturing sectors of East Asian countries that had fostered the industry based on low wages are being shaken by the export offensive of China with its cheap manpower; the excessive depreciation of the Japanese yen; and the strategic devaluation of the Chinese yuan. Even before they were able to develop their own technological capacity and complete industrial restructuring, these countries have lost their strongest advantage of low wages. Therefore, for these countries to restart on the path to growth once more, first and foremost, rapid industrial restructuring is in order. Every East Asian government and company should avoid excessive investment redundancy by specializing in their most competitive industry, based on thorough market principles.

The chain of depreciation in 1997 also had positive effects such as removing bubbles, strengthening export competitiveness, and increasing intraregional trade dependency among Asian countries. To turn the currency crisis into an opportunity, each country needs to make intensive investments in industries appropriate for its development stage and domestic conditions. This would lead to the maximization of the overall competitiveness of the region, enabling the country to enjoy the fruits of efficient intraregional trade.

In order to achieve this, Japan, Korea, Singapore, China and other leading countries in Asia must assume more active role. Asian economies are becoming more and more interdependent: a single country can no longer prosper alone. Therefore East Asian leaders should actively pursue technology transfer and capital investment, thereby promoting the development of neighbouring countries as well as their own. At the same time, each Asian nation should invest more in infrastructure and give the highest priority to education for technological innovation.

Notes

1. Japan, China (including Hong Kong), South Korea, Taiwan, seven ASEAN members, Myanmar, Cambodia, Laos, India, Australia and New Zealand.
2. Figures for seventeen New Asian countries excluding Brunei, Myanmar, Cambodia and Laos.
3. Figures for seventeen New Asian countries excluding Brunei, Myanmar, Cambodia and Laos.
5. In a situation where Japanese-made vehicles have gained over 90 per cent of the market, Indonesia announced its domestic car development plan and joined forces with Kia Motors of South Korea. It is uncertain whether it will succeed, because of many factors including inadequate facilities.
6. In Indonesia, the labour force is increasing by over 3 per cent a year and numbering some 80 million (about 40 per cent of the total population).
7. Malays account for 59 per cent; Chinese, 31 per cent; and Indians, 8 per cent. Non-Malays total 40 per cent. Malays living in Borneo are different from those living on the Malay peninsula. Therefore the actual proportion of Malays in the mainland is about 50 per cent.
8. Around the time when Malaysia attained independence from British rule, it was rich in natural resources, with the production of crude oil, natural gas, wood, rubber and so on making up 80 per cent of the total GDP. However, since unstable prices led to negative growth for the first time in 1985, Indonesia launched the first Industrialization Master Plan (IMP 1) in 1986, mainly targeting the development of manufacturing.
9. Foreign Economic Policy Research Institute (1997) *Regional Economy*, May.
10. Investment attraction delegations led by the Prime Minister visited countries around the globe. As a result, the number of government-approved projects over ten years from 1986 totalled 6956, with contributions from some fifty nations amounting to US$39 billion.
11. Exports of the Philippines' Mactan Export Processing Zone (MEPE) amounted to US$663 million in 1994, 3.9 per cent of total exports. Among importing countries, Japan ranked first with thirty-five businesses, followed by the EU with six, the USA with two, and Taiwan with two consecutively.
12. Wood totals US$33.6 million; rubber, US$21.2 million; and soya beans, US$6 million, respectively.
13. Tobacco and alcohol total US$62.6 million; petroleum products, US$52.8 million; textiles, US$12.3 million; and consumption goods, US$13.7 million.
14. Korea Import-Export Bank (1996) *Sueun Research Monthly*, vol. 1.

15. This policy targets the shift of the socialist economic system to a market system. The aims of this are the prosperity of the nation and the liberalization of all economic and social fields, strengthening the national system for the people.
16. Foreign Economic Policy Research Institute (1997) *Regional Economy*, vol. 5.
17. Singapore was highest with 48.4 per cent followed by UK and Taiwan with 12.7 per cent and 10.6 per cent respectively. The figure for Korea is 0.5 per cent. (Eximbank (1999) *Exim Monthly Magazine*, January.

References

The Economist Intelligence Unit (1997) 'Cambodia', *The Economist.*
The Economist Intelligence Unit (1997) 'Indonesia', *The Economist.*
The Economist Intelligence Unit (1997) 'Laos', *The Economist.*
The Economist Intelligence Unit (1997) 'Malaysia', *The Economist.*
The Economist Intelligence Unit (1997) 'Myanmar', *The Economist.*
The Economist Intelligence Unit (1997) 'Thailand', *The Economist.*
The Economist Intelligence Unit (1997) 'The Philippines', *The Economist.*
The Economist Intelligence Unit (1997) 'Vietnam', *The Economist.*
IMF (1997) *Directory of Trade Statistics Yearbook.*
Korea Import-Export Bank (1996) *Sueun Research Monthly*, vol. 1.
League of Nations (1995) Statistical Yearbook of the League of Nations.
Robert Lloyd George (1992) *The East-West Pendulum* (Simon & Schuster).
Mitsubishi Research Institute (1996) *Total Forecasting of Asia.*

Conclusion

People's enthusiasm for and consent regarding a nation's development are not readily quantifiable. They are, however, important
economic indicators in estimating a nation's economic potential,
and thus are essential elements of economic growth. Accordingly, I
tried to find the roots of the growth energy of Asia in its historical
background and attempted to forecast its future within the framework of a causal nexus of military power, science and technology,
and economic power. From this view, the development energy that
Asian nations have shown so far is truly incredible and, based on
the factors explored in this book, the future looks very promising.
Nevertheless, in the late 1990s Asian economics are being hit hard
enough by plummeting stock prices and currency instability to
be considered part of an 'Asian panic'. Such economic instability
originating from South-east Asian countries is causing concern as to
whether the depletion of the aforementioned development energy is
the cause of the crisis.

Is the Asian economic miracle merely a passing phenomenon produced by massive capital investment, as many economists suggest?
And has it finally reached its limits? Both ideas may be true to some
extent. However, blindly introducing the economic patterns of the
industrialized world would not necessarily have led a less developed
country into high growth. The greatest resource the Asian nations
had were low-wage labour forces characterized by diligence and
outstanding skill. Considering that even the most industrialized
economies have been achieved only after much trial and error, it is
necessary to review the contributing factors and historical meaning

of the Asian economic growth accomplished in such a short period of time. Furthermore, it is erroneous to evaluate growth as merely a passing phenomenon by concentrating on partial problems.

Even when the Japanese economy was at its peak of prosperity, much criticism was levelled against it. Nevertheless, Japan survived great obstacles to become the world's second richest country, and led the paradigm shift of the world's economies. The problems of the Asian economies are that while the disappearance of the low-wage advantage and subsequent industrial restructuring were forecast, Asian nations failed to prepare in advance for political reasons. It is also true that the uninterrupted growth made people overestimate their capabilities. Above all, however, it was the ruling class, which justified its long-term power with high growth, that exaggerated economic success. As a result, the people abandoned the virtue of frugality and became caught up in a spending spree, trying to pick the fruits of growth before they were even ripe.

Asian nations achieved considerable success by following the Japanese model of high growth. However, they, also inherited the side-effects as well. Japan, which first formulated the high growth policy, has suffered from the 'bursting of its bubble', and South Korea, a close follower of Japan, is experiencing similar problems. Now South-east Asian countries are finding themselves in the same predicament.

Since the end of the Second World War, Asia has truly been a furnace of growth. While those living in the midst of it cannot feel the speed, in the future, 'economic explosion' will be the only words to describe Asian economic growth. From a macroeconomic point of view, Asian economies are experiencing the side-effects of restructuring that naturally follow condensed growth. In order to turn the current economic crisis into a passing phenomenon and take off again, Asian countries need to devise a new growth formula as soon as possible to enter a stage of qualitative growth.

To accomplish this, the context and causes of the Asian economic crisis of the late 1990s must be analyzed in depth. The direct causes can be summed up as the decline of export competitiveness; instability of financial systems and growing distrust in the governments; and the inherent problems of Asia's labour division structure. First the decline in export competitiveness is mainly attributable to the excess devaluation of the Japanese yen and the Chinese yuan.[1] In the past, when the yen remained strong against the US dollar, South-east Asian countries, including Thailand, were able to export aggressively to Japan, propelled by the weak dollar. However, since mid-1995, as the value of the yen dropped by 50 per cent against the US dollar, widespread revaluation of currencies ensued, thereby seriously weakening the region's export competitiveness. Second, the instability of the monetary system is a weakness shared by all the countries in Asia. In Asia, the collusive link between political groups, conglomerates and the financial sector is extremely strong, and any attempt to overhaul the ineffective monetary system is likely to fail because of pressure from powerful political groups. Ultimately, this unhealthy link inflicts serious damage on the region's credibility abroad.

Third, the structural problems of Asia's labour division system can be attributed to four factors: (i) Japan's slow economy halted the region's move towards advance industrialization and the speed of technology transfer was reduced even further; (ii) the opening of Japan's markets is far from satisfactory; (iii) China is emerging rapidly as a powerful exporting country by utilizing its position as a global production base; and (iv) the high productivity of ASEAN countries is leading to a serious oversupply. In other words, South-east Asian countries are experiencing the same dilemmas that Korea faced: namely that Korea is trapped between the prolonged slump of the technologically advanced and efficient Japan and the low wages and devalued yuan of China. Unable to compete with China's low prices, and financially burdened with the repayment of principal and interest caused by plummeting currency values, Korea and the leading countries of ASEAN – Indonesia, Malaysia, Thailand and The Philippines – are caught in a double bind.

China jumped into the economic war armed with wages lower than ASEAN members[2] and a weak yuan. China's share in the USA's market, the world's biggest, rocketed from 6 per cent in 1987 to 26 per cent in 1996. Concerned about such offensives from China, foreign investors in South-east Asia decided that the growth potential there was exhausted and diverted their capital to Latin-American markets. Accordingly, South-east Asian countries took action to depreciate their currencies to compete with China. South-east Asian countries, in order to continue to attract development funds, have adopted a fixed exchange rate system and artificially blocked foreign fluctuation. Appropriate reassessment became necessary, but a more fundamental factor, was their belief that exporting is the only way that the Asian economic miracle can be sustained.

As various South-east Asian currencies took a nose-dive, incurring huge currency losses to foreign capital, money flowed out of the region like an ebb tide, resulting in a sudden fall in share prices.[3] Domestic capital in the stock markets joined the selling trend, resulting in the concurrent collapse of exchange rates and share prices. All these factors expedited the loss of foreign capital. Even countries with abundant foreign reserves and relatively solid economics, such as Singapore, Hong Kong and Taiwan, were hit by this foreign currency crisis. Consequently, international investors are rearranging their portfolios, thus adding fuel to the fire.

In July 1997, Thailand, which had maintained the fixed exchange rate system, abandoned the defence of its currency. The plummeting baht led to the downfall of currencies in neighbouring countries, including Malaysia and Indonesia, and share prices in nations such as Singapore and Hong Kong plummeted. These tumbling share prices not only devastated the region but also sent shock waves throughout the world, knocking down share prices in the USA and Europe. At the of writing, global financial markets are in chaos, vivid proof that the world economies have indeed become one.

Several important lessons can be learnt from the currency–monetary crisis in South-east Asia. First, the influx of foreign capital can contribute to economic growth only when it improves overall productivity, and short-term foreign funds should be avoided at all costs. Second, during the 1990s, the world's markets have become more and more global, and large amounts of capital have moved across borders with increasing speed, thereby causing instability in monetary systems and the micro economy. Developing countries in particular should focus on restructuring their weak financial infrastructure and implement measures to overhaul their economic structure rather than pursue the liberalization of capital trade. Third, with the development of information technology, the foreign currency markets and the financial markets of advanced countries are, in effect, moving as one. Therefore, risk management system should be strengthened with various measures such as revamping the future market. Fourth, as the exchange rates between major currencies, including the dollar, the yen, and the Deutschemark fluctuate wildly and global money remains in a state of influx, it is risky to implement a fixed exchange rate system linked to a particular currency such as the US dollar. A monetary policy based on a stable linkage to several leading currencies should be pursued. The most fundamental reason for the current financial crisis in East Asia is that the size of the currency economy (US$250 trillion) grew disproportionately large compared to the size of the object-economy (US$5.4 trillion). The distorted growth of the currency economy was caused in large part by the USA. Using the strong note-issuing power of the dollar as leverage, the USA sought to gain substantial control over the currency economy. The markets in Europe are linked by a single monetary unit, the 'euro' while the leading currency in North and South America is the US dollar. Therefore, Asian countries should also create a single, intraregional currency or establish a co-operative network among the central banks in the region, thereby, encouraging co-operation between the various markets.

In this vein, an economic policy where a certain country attempts to prosper alone is no longer effective. Japan, in particular, should more actively transfer its technology to South-east Asian nations. This is not to nurture future competitors but to lay the foundations for selling higher value-added products as well as to create a new demand and boost national competitiveness by restructuring the industry.

China should also develop an economic policy with its Asian neighbours that is mutually beneficial rather than to try to dominate regional economies with its huge domestic market and low wages. In China, every province is competitively attracting foreign capital to foster import-substitution industries. With regard to home appliances such as refrigerators and washing machines, for example, the supply of middle- and low-technology products made within China have already far outstripped demand. If such surplus products flood the global markets at low prices, huge market disturbances will occur.

China seems to be emulating the 'chaebol' (conglomerate) system and import-substitution industries of South Korea that have accomplished condensed growth. However, China's situation is different from South Korea's, and in fact there is much scepticism about whether the South Korean model is still effective. If the situation remains unchanged, Japan, with its advanced technology, will still be able to create new markets to some extent. However, the manufacturing base of the entire Asian region, with the exception of Japan and a handful of other countries, will be on the verge of collapsing.

In the midst of China's indiscriminate export offensive and the counter-offensive of South-east Asia, currencies are tumbling, sending a ripple effect even as far as Hong Kong, South Korea and Taiwan. At the time of writing, prices of competitively exported products are falling, resulting in a deterioration in trading conditions. From a short-term perspective, such price reduction have the effect of lowering real estate and consumer prices as well as removing bubbles from stock markets. However, if the reduction is prolonged, the Asian economies will fall into a situation of reduction and retreat. In fact, export prices of silk, semiconductors and motor vehicles have already fallen drastically. In particular, if such price reductions combine with basic structural problems, such as oversupply caused by prolonged investment in Asia, a destructive competition of price reduction will occur.

The second task is to analyze the export-led economic policy based on low wages. Once their economies grew to some extent, Asian countries spent more and began real estate speculation instead of developing technology and boosting productivity. In the late 1980s, in particular, low-interest Japanese capital[4] flowed in to ASEAN nations, including Thailand and Indonesia. This capital was funnelled into consumption industries and the real estate sector rather than into the production industries, thereby raising real estate prices by as much as 50–100 per cent. While real estate speculation improved the landscape dramatically, the economies began to rot from within. South-east Asia in particular, was under authoritarian rule in the form of 'dictatorship for the sake of development'. In many cases, governments ignored economic logic and engaged in ostentatious administrative policies, including intervening in setting exchange rates. Also, the soaring prices of financial assets, such as stocks and shares, and real estate, an aftermath of rapid growth, formed bubbles in the economies. While the high growth continued, the economies appeared to roll along, but as 'external factors' slowed down the growth, they are being crippled by the side-effects of irrational economic policies and the bursting of bubbles.

To resolve the economic crisis triggered by unstable exchange rates, the International Monetary Fund (IMF), the World Bank (IBRD), the Asian Development Ban (ADB) and others provided a huge amount in loans to Indonesia, South Korea and so on. As Asian currency instability showed signs of spreading to the whole world, major countries, including the USA and Japan, decided to provide active support. Meanwhile, Asian nations are also making sincere efforts to resolve the crisis, for example by pushing for the establishment of an Asian Monetary Fund (AMF) to stabilize intraregional financial markets. Therefore, the role of the ADB will be greatly magnified and in addition, I suggest the establishment of a World Monetary Union (WMU), and the adoption of an Asian version of a single currency similar to the euro embraced by the European Monetary Union (EMU). Such long-term measures are important, but what is urgently needed, most of all, is fundamental economic reform to cure the structural weaknesses of Asian countries which make them vulnerable to even the smallest impacts.

In the late 1990s world economies are showing a contradictory trend of globalizing and localizing at the same time. However, as we have witnessed in the South-east Asian economic crisis, world economies are operating as a single unit and this trend will be increasingly intensified. In this context, rather than adopting the Asia Free Trade Agreement (AFTA), Asian countries should pursue a more wide-ranging and comprehensive arrangement such as the World Free Trade Agreement (WORFTA). In this way, they will be able to implement 'open regionalism' by embracing all countries that share the principle of global economic integration, regardless of region. This is the reason why I have proposed the establishment of a WMU (World Monetary Union) rather than an AMU (Asian Monetary Union).

In this context, the embracing of Far Eastern Russia into Asia will be a good example that reflects the openness of the regional common market. Far Eastern Russia is a huge area comprising 36.4 per cent of the total Russian land mass, and Far East Russians comprise 74.8 per cent of the total population of 8 million. Emotionally, Russians tend to identify with Europeans so, as with Australia and New Zealand, it is difficult to categorize Russia culturally as an Asian nation. Nevertheless, Far Eastern Russia is richly endowed with natural resources and, as a bridge between Europe and Asia, it is economically and geographically important. As the volume of trade with Asia increases and economic dependency on Asia grows stronger as a result, the Russian government is making an effort to include the Far Eastern region in the sphere of Asian economic development. Therefore, it is only a matter of time before Far Eastern Russia becomes a part of the New Asian common market. A series of economic confusions recently erupting in Asia, as detailed above, basically stemmed from the fact that various artificial factors such as political confrontation, borders and tariffs blocked general global trends toward 'one market' and 'one monetary unit'. Therefore, Asian countries, with Japan, Korea and China leading the way, should establish the WORFTA and create a single currency, the WMU, as soon as possible.

Asia has already become the world's largest economic sphere. Only harmony and solidarity among its countries will enable Asia to emerge as a global economic centre in the twenty-first century. Then Asia will be able to contribute to global economic integration and subsequently to the economic equality and prosperity of humankind.

Notes

1. The Chinese government depreciated the yuan by up to 35 per cent in early 1994.
2. The wage per hour in China in 1997 was US$0.9, far lower than the US$1.8 in Indonesia; US$4.6 in Malaysia; US$1.3 in The Philippines; US$3.0 in Thailand; and US$6.2 in South Korea.
3. The Morgan Stanley Index (MSCI), a criterion for the investment ratio of global fund in emerging markets, clearly shows the departure of foreigners from Asia. The investment ratio in Hong Kong shrank from 3.2 per cent at the end of May 1997 to 1.7 per cent at the end of September of the same year; in Singapore, from 1.3 per cent to 0.5 per cent; and in Thailand, from 0.4 per cent to 0.2 per cent respectively, which in total decreased by half.
4. The interest rate for loans that ASEAN banks made to businesses of member nations was about 16 per cent while it was only 5 per cent for yen funds.

Index